EXPERIENCING SCRIPTURE IN WORLD RELIGIONS

FAITH MEETS FAITH

An Orbis Series in Interreligious Dialogue

Paul F. Knitter, General Editor

In the contemporary world, the many religions and spiritualities stand in need of greater communication and cooperation. More than ever before, they must speak to, learn from, and work with each other in order to maintain their vital identities and to contribute to fashioning a better world.

The FAITH MEETS FAITH Series seeks to promote interreligious dialogue by providing an open forum for exchange among followers of different religious paths. While the Series wants to encourage creative and bold responses to questions arising from contemporary appreciations of religious plurality, it also recognizes the multiplicity of basic perspectives concerning the methods and content of interreligious dialogue.

Although rooted in a Christian theological perspective, the Series does not limit itself to endorsing any single school of thought or approach. By making available to both the scholarly community and the general public works that represent a variety of religious and methodological viewpoints, FAITH MEETS FAITH seeks to foster an encounter among followers of the religions of the world on matters of common concern.

Faith Meets Faith Series

EXPERIENCING SCRIPTURE IN WORLD RELIGIONS

edited by

Harold Coward

ORBIS BOOKS

Maryknoll, New York 10545

The Catholic Foreign Mission Society of America (Maryknoll) recruits and trains people for overseas missionary service. Through Orbis Books, Maryknoll aims to foster the international dialogue that is essential to mission. The books published, however, reflect the opinions of their authors and are not meant to represent the official position of the society. To obtain more information about Maryknoll and Orbis Books, please visit our website at www.maryknoll.org.

Published by Orbis Books, Maryknoll, New York, U.S.A.

Manufactured in the United States of America.
Copy editing and typesetting by Joan Weber Laflamme.

Library of Congress Cataloging-in-Publication Data

Experiencing scripture in world religions / edited by Harold Coward.
p. cm. — (Faith meets faith series)
Includes bibliographical references and index.
ISBN 1-57075-298-2 (paper)
1. Sacred books—Devotional use. I. Coward, Harold G. II. Faith meets faith.

BL71.E96 2000
291.8'2—dc21

99-058570

Contents

PREFACE ix

INTRODUCTION 1
Harold Coward

The Spiritual Power of Spoken Scripture 1
Contemporary Life and the Sacred Word 6

1. JUDAISM 15
Eliezer Segal

Hillel and the Two Torahs 15
A Tale of Two Festivals 16
Pharisees, Sadducees, and Ancestral Traditions 19
Lunar and Solar Calendars 21
Midrash: The Oral Tradition Interprets the Written 23
Scripture in the Synagogue 23
Torah in Daily Life 27
Interpreting the Commandments 29
Eternally New 30

2. THE NATURE AND FUNCTION OF ORAL AND WRITTEN SCRIPTURE FOR THE CHRISTIAN DEVOTEE 34
Wayne O. McCready

Scripture and Christianity—An Introduction 34
Features of Scripture 35
Scripture, Origins of Christianity and Its Development 37
Origins of Christianity 37
The Old Testament 38
The Old Testament and the Christian Devotee 40

The New Testament and the Origins of Christianity Revisited *43*
The New Testament and the Christian Devotee *49*
Scripture and the Monastic Traditions *52*
Sermons, Liturgy, Architecture, and Art *54*
Scripture, the Protestant Reformation, and Modern Christianity *56*
Conclusion 59

3. **THE QUR'ĀN** **63**
Hanna Kassis

The Revelation and the Messenger: "Say…'this Koran has been revealed to me that I may warn you thereby'" (6:19) 64
Communicating the Message: "O Messenger, deliver that which has been sent down to thee from thy Lord" (5:67) 67
The Language of the Qur'ān: "We have sent it down as an Arabic Qur'ān" (12:2) 69
Structure: "A Book whose verses are set clear, and then distinguished" (11:1) 70
The Canon of the Qur'ān: "Nay, but it is a glorious Koran, in a guarded tablet" (85:21-22) 72
The "Vulgate"—Uthmān's Recension: "A Book sent down to thee—so let there be no impediment in thy breast because of it—to warn thereby, and as a reminder to believers" (7:2) 76
The Liturgical Use of the Qur'ān: "Those to whom We have given the Book recite it with true recitation" (2:121) 78

4. **HINDUISM** **85**
Anantanand Rambachan

Mokṣa: The Highest Goal of Human Life 86
Artha, Kāma *and* Dharma *as Secondary Goals* *87*
Mokṣa *as Liberation from* Avidyā *87*
Mokṣa *as Liberation from* Karma *and* Saṁsāra *88*
Oral and Written Scripture 88
Śruti *and* Smṛti *88*

The Vedas as *Śruti* 89
The Four Vedas 89
The Authority of the Vedas 91
The Six Vedāṇgas 93
Smṛti: The Remembered Scriptures 94
Itiḥasa *95*
Rāmāyaṇa *96*
Purāṇas *97*
Āgamas *and* Tantras *97*
Sacred Literature in the Vernacular 98
The Experience of Scripture in the Life of the Devotee 99
Memorization and Repetition of Scripture 99
The Use of Scripture in Ritual 100
The Use of Scripture for Japa 101
The Use of Scripture as a Valid Source of Knowledge (Pramāṇa) *102*
Pūrva Mīmāṁsā *and* Uttara Mīmāṁsā *103*
The Rāmāyaṇa *as* Līlā *(Play) 107*
The Rāmāyaṇa *as* Kathā *108*
Rāmāyaṇa *as Television Drama 108*

5. **SIKHISM** **113**
Harjot Oberoi

The "Forgotten Tradition" 115
The Structure and Language of the *Guru Granth Sahib* 121
The Power of the Revealed Word in the Sikh Tradition 124
An Ethnography of *Rites de Passage* and the Sacred Text 130
Conclusions 133

6. **THE DILEMMA OF AUTHORITATIVE UTTERANCE IN BUDDHISM** **138**
Eva K. Neumaier

The Dilemma 138
What Is Buddhism? 139
The Origins: The Buddha 139

The Dharma 140
The "Word of the Buddha" 142
The Canons 142
Scripture Embedded in Oral Tradition 157
Multiplicity of the Dharma 159
The Word of the Buddha as Silence 161
Denial of a Teachable Dharma 161
The Great Perfection: Atiyoga 161
Ch'an / Zen Buddhism 164
Concluding Thoughts 164

ABOUT THE AUTHORS **169**

INDEX **171**

Preface

The chapters in this book evolved from lectures given in the annual Distinguished Speakers Series organized by the Centre for Studies in Religion and Society and co-sponsored by the University of Victoria's Division of Continuing Studies.

The Centre for Studies in Religion and Society was established at the University of Victoria in 1991 to foster the scholarly study of religion in relation to the sciences, ethics, social and economic development, and other aspects of culture. The primary aim is to promote dialogue between religion and these other aspects of human experience. The Centre has a fundamental commitment to pluralism and pursues a broad range of research interests not limited to any specific time, place, religion, or culture. It embodies the understanding that religious traditions have been formative of human reality and experience, and that they are the proper object of creative, rigorous inquiry, whether from a disciplinary or an interdisciplinary perspective.

Each year the Centre invites distinguished scholars from various religions to speak on a common theme from the perspective of their own traditions. The 1999 Distinguished Speakers Series on Oral and Written Scripture in World Religions evoked such strong and positive audience response that they were augmented and revised for publication as a book.

Thanks are due to the Centre's Administrator, Ludgard De Decker, for her careful preparation of the manuscript. As always, it has been a pleasure to work with William Burrows and his staff at Orbis Books in the publishing of this volume.

Harold Coward
Director
Centre for Studies in Religion and Society
University of Victoria
Victoria, British Columbia, Canada

Introduction

Harold Coward

In all religions the scriptural word is seen as a means of revealing or realizing the Divine. However, this spiritual power of the word is most often located in the oral rather than the written form of scripture. It is the spoken sound that effectively evokes the Divine. The written word, when read silently, may share in some of this power if the silent reading results in the mental hearing of the words being spoken. A reading of the words for intellectual analytical purposes, with little or no sense of oral reverberation in the mind, seems not to take one to the Divine. Yet it is through union or communion with the Divine that one's consciousness is transformed and the deepest religious experience realized.

THE SPIRITUAL POWER OF SPOKEN SCRIPTURE

Of the spoken words, some seem to have more evocative power than others. Poetic scripture is experienced as more powerful than prose scripture. In Hinduism, for example, the Vedic hymns, which take the form of poems spoken by the *ṛsis* or seers, are the primary scriptures. The later prose Brahmanas and Upaniṣads serve to exegete the fundamental insights contained in the Vedic poems. In ritual and devotional practice it is the poetic words of the Vedas that are chanted. Of the secondary Hindu scripture *(smṛti)*, it is the epic poetry of the *Bhagavada Gita* and the Ramayana, along with the poems of poet-saints such as Manikkavacakar in the South and Kabir in the North, that are learned by heart in the childhood and chanted devotionally throughout life. This oral performance of scriptural poetry can take the form of individual chanting as in morning and evening prayers, or group singing of the poems as hymns of *kirtan*. Great emphasis is placed upon the correct use of accent, meter, and melody in the chanting, so that the spoken form will "match up with" or evoke the divine Word of which it is an earthly resonance. It is because of this perceived resonance between the uttered sound and the Transcendent that Hindu practice prescribes the repeated chanting. A direct correspondence is seen as existing between the physical vibrations of the phenomenal chant and the noumenal vibrations of the Transcendent. The more the physical vibrations of the uttered chant are repeated, the more Transcendent power is evoked in experience until one's consciousness is purified and transformed. It is this principle that is behind the practice of the repeated chanting of mantras or scripture verses in Hinduism. A technical description of this purification process is offered in *The Yoga-system of Patanjali*.[1] Special symbolic scriptural words, such as AUM, are judged to have particular power. They are said to be the "seed forms" or fundamental sounds out of which all others arise. Thus, chants such as AUM are taken as symbolically including within themselves, in potential form, all other scriptural sounds. The repetition of AUM, then, provides a "shorthand" technique of chanting all scripture in one syllable. The vibration produced by chanting AUM is seen to equate with the primal manifestation of *Daivi Vāk*, the divine Word, in its descent from the Divine into the human realm. In the Sikh tradition, the devotional chanting of *Nām* fulfills a similar function.

Buddhism shares with Hinduism this notion of oral recitation of scripture as a sanctifying and sacramental act.[2] The memorization of a text, although an important prerequisite, is not the most important aspect of oral practice. It is the different mode of perception involved in the oral performance of scripture that is crucial. By chanting or listening to the rhythmic words of a sacred text, the teaching and inspiration in the words are renewed and reinforced. In Tibetan Buddhism, for example, the chanting of the Tantric syllables OM MA NE PA ME HUM accompanied by the performing of ritual gestures enables the monks to feel the evocation of overtones of the interdependence of the universe—a meaning that can be said symbolically in the chanted sounds and gestures but not said explicitly. The evoking of the symbolic overtones is the more powerful by virtue of the fact that the monks chant the tantric syllables not in monotone but in chords—with each monk actually chanting a D major chord, D-F#-A, simultaneously.[3] The felt experience of the resonance of the chanted chord within one's own voice box powerfully induces numinous sensations throughout one's whole being.

In Jodo Shinshu Buddhism also, ritual chanting is the major means of spiritual practice. Finding that rational study of Buddhist texts was not helpful, Shinran, the founder of Jodo Shinshu, taught his followers that one sincere chanting of the *nembutsu* ("Namu Amida Buddha") was the means by which enlightenment could be realized. Although the rational meaning of the chant may be "I surrender myself to Amida Buddha," it is through the power of the chant to evoke emotional, intuitive, and memory-laden processes that the existential experience of oneness with Amida Buddha is realized. As one Buddhist priest puts it: "The chant has the function of structuring spiritual space: the sound of the chant, the smell of incense, and the action of putting hands together—all this through repeated experience becomes predictable and induces the spiritual."[4] Shinran urged his followers to chant the *nembutsu* aloud, rather than chanting the text quietly within, if its full spiritual power was to be felt.

The Buddhist tradition, following Hindu practice, has always used oral chanting (both group and individual) as a device for embedding scripture in the budding consciousness of the young child. First the scripture is memorized by being repeated aloud after the teacher, and only after that is it studied analytically for its rational meaning. But discursive academic study is always of secondary importance, since knowledge of the Transcendent can never be fully captured and communicated in words. Spiritual transformation takes place more through the continuous action of the memorized words, which have become a part of the very structure of consciousness, than through intellectual study. The poetic power of the words to point beyond themselves and resonate strongly with the Transcendent is a major force in the religious transformation of consciousness. In addition, the permanent presence of the memorized scripture within consciousness makes it constantly available for guidance, inspiration, and solace in the crisis moments of life.

In Sikhism the scripture, the Adi Granth, is seen to be the living guru or teacher who gives guidance daily in response to the perplexing problems of life. By the ritual practice of the *vak lao*, taking the advice of the word, Sikhs look to their scripture for guidance as one would look to a living guru. Just as a guru through divine knowledge of the contemporary situation would choose the right portion of God's truth to speak to that problem, so divine inspiration operates through a ritual in which the priest (or the devotee) opens the text of the Adi Granth at random and begins reading from the first verse on the top left page. This word, when spoken, is received by the devotee as God's will or commandment for that moment, day, or situation in life. *Vak lao* occurs in every service of worship, in individual daily devotions, in the *Amrit* or initiation ceremony (into wearing the turban and other sacred symbols), in the naming of one's child, in marriage, and in death. For Sikhs, it is fundamental means of spiritual transformation.

Judaism emphasizes the early learning of the scriptural words and then their ritual repetition throughout life. The *shema* is taught to the children at an early age and chanted by the whole family in the morning and evening. Elementary schooling provided by the community to children is devoted largely to learning sacred Hebrew language and to becoming capable of reading the written Torah in public. To do so virtually requires that the text be known by heart, since the synagogue Torah text is unpointed (i.e., lacking vowels) and in the early texts the consonant letters were not divided into words. Thus to read the text correctly, prior knowledge of what the text is saying is required so that the letters can be correctly divided into words and sentences with the correct vowels being inserted.[5] In addition to learning to read the written Torah in the Jewish elementary school, the students then went on to the advanced school, where the oral Torah was taught. Even in the Yeshivas or seminaries, study of the scripture traditionally proceeded by group chanting of the words so that they became deeply ingrained in the students' consciousness. Once the basic memorization of both written and oral texts was completed, exegesis would be begun, but this too was in the form of oral discourse between teacher and students.

A similar oral practice seems to have been followed by Jesus and his apostles, who grew up as Jews within functioning Jewish communities. Thus the early memorizing of the written Torah along with the oral traditions of the teachings and acts of Jesus was the norm for Christian practice for the first few decades. Even when the teachings of Jesus were written down in gospels between 60 and 100 C.E., these gospels were not written to be read as books in individual study, as is usually done today. Rather, they, like the letters of Paul and the Revelation of John, were written as scripts for oral performance in public worship. Like the Torah or Old Testament, they were read in oral performance by skilled orators before the whole congregation. It was through the repeated hearing and remembering of the oral scriptural words that they became deeply rooted within the psyches of children and adults alike.

Islam not only adopted the tradition of oral memorization and repeating of scripture, but if anything pursued the spoken word with even greater rigor and intensity. Indeed, spiritual merit in Islam is said to be measured by the thoroughness of one's oral knowledge of the scripture. According to the tradition, on the day of resurrection everyone will be called upon to rise up and recite the Qur'ān. For each verse that is correctly recited, the person rises up one station in heavenly merit. If the whole of the text can be recited, the devotee is said to be like a prophet and to share in the rewards of everlasting life in paradise.[6] The memorization and later recitation of the Qur'ān were required of Muhammad by God, and they are likewise the expectation of every pious Muslim. Thus a complete recitation of the Qur'ān brings spiritual merit and is a time of celebration. The memorized Qur'ān is the faithful companion and guide that enables the Muslim to journey through this life and into the hereafter. For its full power, the Qur'ān is recited according to various traditions of musical chant that seek to show forth the incomparable beauty of the divinely composed words. The truth of the words is seen to be verified by the aesthetic beauty of the poetic form and sound of the musically chanted Arabic Qur'ān—which, it is claimed, surpasses all other experiences of poetry, either secular or sacred. But fully to experience that beauty, it is essential that the listener already know the text—just as the full experience of a Bach fugue requires a complete familiarity of a kind that can only be realized from the repeated hearing and playing of the fugue. Just as such a performance of the fugue must be done without a musical score so that there is nothing between the performer and the music, allowing a complete loss of the artist in the music, so also the full experience of living life in scripture requires that the text be known by heart so that one can lose oneself in it.

CONTEMPORARY LIFE AND THE SACRED WORD

Learning the scriptures by heart while one is young, and then repeatedly chanting them throughout the course of one's adult life, are requirements built into all six of the major religions examined. It is a requirement which, when followed, gives to scriptural words the power of transforming lives. It is strange today that our pedagogy, within modern religion as well as within our school curricula, has moved in the opposite direction. While we agree with music teachers that our children need to learn their pieces by heart for full mastery of the music, yet, in the modern West at least, we have given way to educational approaches that have given up the need for memorization and are content with the literary skills of being able to find the Bible in the library, use its table of contents, and have some knowledge of its literary sources and the sociocultural background they reflect. Descriptive knowledge of the scripture rather than intimate acquaintance with the scripture has too often become the accepted standard for scriptural study.

In this modern context frequently more time is spent in reading *about* scripture than in the firsthand reading of scripture itself—let alone any expectation that the scripture should be memorized. As a result, for most moderns, scripture has ceased to be the guiding companion of life that resides in one's deepest layers of consciousness, influencing one even when one is not aware of its presence. Instead, scripture has become a literary object to be studied and analyzed along with the other literary texts we possess. Not only is scripture lost to us as the grounding source of our individual thought and behavior, but no longer does it function as the baseline of our corporate or communal consciousness. We have recognized that it is important to train our children in classical music through hard hours of practice and often against their own wishes. As parents we have persisted with such training in the conviction that it is essential if our children are to participate in, enjoy, and value the music that we have received as an important part of our culture. Yet as parents and teachers we have given up the same requirements for the teaching of scripture to our children, even though down through the histories of our religious traditions it is the deep immersion in scripture that has provided the foundational source of religious experience.

While the above comments apply most obviously to the modern Western Christian experience (especially Protestant), the same thing can be seen to be happening to the other religions as they encounter the challenge of having to live within the context of modernity. In Islamic Egypt, for example, Islamic teachers became alarmed at the decreasing memorization of the oral Qur'ān by young children and the falling off of good teachers and reciters. In response a project was initiated to record the chanted Qur'ān on audio records as a way of preserving the oral text and in the hope that this recording would be used by Muslims all over the world in the education of their young. Such a common chanted Qur'ān, it was hoped, would maintain the common spiritual basic that in the past had bound together the Muslims of all countries and cultures.[7]

Similar worries have arisen in Hindu communities. Analysis of the experience in Hindu families that have emigrated to North America suggests that the parents are ineffective in transmitting their oral experience of scripture to their children, and that even in the parents' own spiritual discipline shortcuts are sought to replace traditional morning and evening recitation of scripture. For many, instead of setting aside one or two hours in the morning and evening to chant passages from the scriptures in Sanskrit, all of this has been replaced by the chanting of the guru's name 108 time two or three times a day. The rationale for this practice is that it can be done successfully in the context of the fast pace of modern life—which, unlike the slower pace of India, leaves little leisure for lengthy devotional exercises. It also gets around the problem of having to maintain and pass on knowledge of Sanskrit to one's children. Since learning Sanskrit and the proper melodic forms of chanting verses seems to be out of the question in North America, and since most agree that English translations do not "vibrate correctly," the solution adopted appears to be the use of a very simple chant in the original Sanskrit language—such as the repetition of the guru's Sanskrit name.[8] Adults who do engage in the serious study of scriptures are often led by modern scholarship to do so by using written texts in English, which follow a literary-critical rather than a devotional-oral approach.

Modern Buddhist communities also report a shift away from traditional oral chant and toward the rational presentation of scripture through sermon and printed book. The worry expressed by some Buddhists is that this shift may have the effect of cutting off the Buddhist consciousness from its spiritual root. If Buddhist scripture is not learned in childhood through ritual repetition, if the oral teachings are not nourished and reinforced in adulthood by private and public repetition, then the spiritual foundation they provide within the psyche will be missing, and sermons and the study of books may become empty exercises. In the Jodo Shinshu tradition it is held that the unity and harmony found within a congregation can be measured by monitoring its chanting.[9] In a Protestant context it may well be that a similar evaluation can be made based on the way the congregation sings its hymns.

The above Buddhist analysis makes an important point. It is not the case that written-down and read scriptures and sermons are always empty of spiritual power. The point being made is that when scripture is learned and nourished *only* through written and read materials, without an underlying oral foundation having been established and maintained, *then* the written scripture will be empty of spiritual power. Such scripture would be like a written poem that may be taken up and read from time to time but never becomes a part of the reader's consciousness in such a way that the written text is transcended. Until the poem takes shape and roots itself in one's consciousness, its words lack the power to move one. It is the contention of the oral traditions that for such "rooting within consciousness" to take place, the words must shift from the visual sense (the objective perception of an external form) to the oral-aural sense (the subjective experience of a living word with which one can strongly identify).

This traditional contention is supported by Jacques Ellul, who finds the printed word to be of a nature entirely different from that of the spoken word. His thesis is that our modern experience biases us toward printed words, which function as signs with fixed factual referents (information). Spoken words, on the other hand, function as symbols that cannot be reduced to factual information but necessarily involve emotions that transcend reflexes and rationality and overflow into breadth of meaning, ambiguity, and paradox.[10] Ellul is not seeking to despise the written word and its function but rather to point out that the written word belongs to a different realm of truth and to refuse to reduce spoken language to the written realm. Ellul realizes that in reality the two realms of written and the oral overlap. His complete separation of the two is only for the purposes of conceptual analysis. A protest similar to that of Ellul's was mounted by Paul in his contrast between the oral and the written word. In 2 Corinthians 3:3 ("show that you are a letter from Christ delivered by us, written not with ink, but with the Spirit of the living God, not on the tablets of stone, but on tablets of the human heart") it is the embodied and spoken word that manifests the living Spirit of God, as opposed to the word written with ink. Paul's point, like Ellul's, is that for the word to have transforming power it must be "written," not on paper or stone, but on the human heart. Paul, of course, does not originate this polarity but picks it up from the Hebrew Bible, where the prophet Jeremiah reports God as saying that to redeem his people he must make a new covenant with them: "I will put my law within them, I will write it upon their hearts" (Jer 31:33).

Luther valued the written word to the extent of dedicating much of his life to translating the Bible into German so that it could be read aloud in services of worship and so orally enter the German-speaking consciousness of the people. But, for Luther, it was the spoken and preached scripture that had power to transform lives, not the bare printed text. Even when orally encountered, however, it is the action of the Holy Spirit within one that allows the good news of the spoken word to take possession of one's life and be understood.[11] The English King James Version accomplished the same goal for English-speaking people. The printed text was to serve only to provide for the powerful oral performance of the word, which was to be followed by preaching. The Puritans of England and North America gave further stress to Luther's emphasis upon the presence and action of the Holy Spirit in preaching. They saw printed and mechanically read sermons as obstructions that served to "kill" rather than proclaim the good news. In order for the scripture to speak through them, preachers had to submit to the impulse of the Holy Spirit and allow it to lead them into fresh oral exposition. Preaching of the "lively word," as the Puritans called it, required freedom from a printed text so that the inspiration of the Holy Spirit within both the preacher and the hearers could take possession of the process.[12] The presence of large portions of memorized scripture in the consciousness of the preacher and the hearers surely paves the way for this spontaneous and inspiring functioning of the Holy Spirit. The lack of power in many modern sermons may well be due, at least in part, to the lack of this reservoir of scriptural knowledge as held in common by both the preacher and the congregation. Perhaps the reason one hears from the pulpit so many allusions to television programs is because TV, rather than scripture, provides the pool of knowledge that is held in common today. Surely this must make it difficult for even the Holy Spirit to make such sermons into inspiring preaching. Jesus, himself, had the advantage in his teaching of sharing with his listeners the "oral pool" of the Hebrew scripture. It would seem, then, that for the scriptural word, whether spoken from memory or read aloud from a book, to be proclaimed with transforming power requires that to some degree it be already present in the consciousness of the hearer and the speaker.

In the Eastern experience the presupposition of knowledge being already present in consciousness functions in somewhat different ways. While the Hindu Vedas used the poetic form to evoke the Divine, the Upaniṣads take the form of prose dialogues between teacher and students in which the teacher frequently employs a *via negativa*. Instead of using the spoken words of dialogue to convey positive knowledge of Truth, the teacher allows students to produce their own characterizations and then negates them with the intention of leading the student from surface identifications (e.g., outward appearance is true reality) to progressively deeper realizations (e.g., consciousness itself is the ultimate reality) until finally in a flash of insight the student has the direct experience of that which transcends and yet makes possible all conceptualizations. The scriptural words, by a series of negations, lead beyond themselves, and, in the final negation, reveal the fullness of the Transcendent in direct experience.[13]

Madhymika Buddhism tends to see language and conceptualization as an obstruction to the realization of the Transcendent. Again a *via negativa* is adopted. Language is used to criticize and demonstrate the inability of language to encapsulate ultimate truth.[14] Words in this context have no positive spiritual content but can play the negative function of removing other words that are blocking the realization of the spiritual power already present in consciousness. The Chinese and Japanese version of this Buddhist use of language as a *via negativa* is found in koan practice. As an illogical or absurd use of words, a koan makes no pretense of expressing the inexpressible Transcendent. Rather, its aim is to convince the mind to give up its ego-directed attempt to reach the Transcendent through the use of words and logic. Koan meditation does not itself evoke enlightenment. Rather, it negates the ego-centered word use of the mind, thus clearing the way for the spontaneous arising of the *satori* or enlightenment experience.[15] But even this negative use of words as koans is rejected by Soto Zen Buddhism. For Soto Zen, silent meditation (*zazen*) alone is the trustworthy path to enlightenment. Through silent meditation the ego-attachment to words will gradually dissipate within the mind until no word forms remain. As one Zen master puts it, through meditation the mind is vacuum-cleaned of the word-concepts that are obstructing its pure flow. All that remains is "silence," the primal stillness of the ground of the enlightened mind, whose natural activity is to "shine".[16] The silent, shining, unclouded mind clearly mirrors reality, and this, for the Buddhist, is the Transcendent realization.

With the exception of the forms of Buddhism just mentioned, the holy words of scripture are experienced within all religions as having spiritual power. The recitation of the holy word not only purifies the life of the individual devotee but is also often seen to be necessary for the well-being of the rest of humanity and the maintenance of order in nature. The recitation and preaching of the word evokes the truth of the Divine, which transcends all words. To this end the scriptural forms that seem to have the greatest power are those of poem, parable, and *via negativa* dialogue. But in all of these, it is the oral rather than the written word in which the full spiritual power is present. It is the oral word experienced within the context of preacher and listener, guru and student, and in chanted prayer or meditation that has been found to have the power to transform lives. The written word alone seems largely empty of such power. But when used as a script for oral practice, the written word through the oral joins in the production of spiritual power. In certain situations the written word is seen to have made possible the production of oral experiences that, without the use of the written, might never have occurred (e.g., the writing of the gospels for subsequent oral performance).

The written text also provides the basis for the investigation of past events as history and the abstract analysis and classification of scripture.[17] Except in classical Greece and India, the writing down of a scriptural text has usually given it special authority and at times made it an object of veneration. Copies of sacred books (the Bible, the Qur'ān, and the Buddhist Sūtras) were popularly used for divination and as talismans possessing magical powers.[18] In earlier times, as van der Leeuw points out, writing also functioned as magic, as a way of gaining power over the living word. Committing the oral scripture to writing was an act of power in that it enabled humans to do what they wanted with the written word.[19] The great danger in modern life, with its strong bias toward the written and its lack of awe before the written copy of any text, is that the oral experience of scripture will be reduced to the written and the transforming power of the word will no longer be experienced.

With the notable exception of Hinduism, the awe and respect traditionally given to written scripture are well evidenced in the pious copying and special ornamentation of the Bible, the exquisite beauty of Qur'ān calligraphy, the elegant block print collections of the Tibetan texts, and the special qualifications and purifications involved in the scribe's copying of the Torah. All of this has traditionally functioned to set written scripture apart from other writing and to highlight its special symbolic qualities. However, in our modern culture, with its surfeit of written materials, the printing of the scripture in the latest paperback style leads to a familiarity that lessens any sense of separateness or special quality. This loss of awe is reinforced when we study the scriptures by subjecting them to the same kinds of literary-critical analysis that would be given to any other piece of writing. As a result of all of this, there is the strong danger that written scripture will be redefined as nothing but sign language referencing empirical objects, that its intimate relation to oral performance will be lost sight of, and that the ability of scripture to act as an evocative symbol of the Transcendent with the power to transform lives will be lost.

The following chapters describe and analyze the experience of oral and written scripture in the lives of Jews, Christians, Muslims, Hindus, Buddhists and Sikhs.

Notes

[1] *The Yoga-system of Patanjali*, trans. J. H Woods, Harvard Oriental Series, vol. 17 (Delhi: Motilal Banarsidass, 1966), 1:27-28, 42-44, and 11:32.

[2] Joseph Kitagawa, "Some Remarks on the Study of Sacred Texts," in *The Critical Study of Sacred Texts,* ed. Wendy Doniger O'Flaherty (Berkeley: Religious Studies Series, 1979), 235.

[3] See the film "Requiem for a Faith" by Huston Smith (Cos Cob, Conn.: Hartley Film Foundation, 1986).

[4] David J. Goa and Harold G. Coward, "Sacred Ritual, Sacred Language: Jodo Shinshu Religious Forms in Transition," *Studies in Religion, 12* (1983), 363-79.

[5] "Torah, Reading of," *Encyclopedia Judaica* (New York: Macmillan, 1971-72), 1254.

[6] Mahmoud Ayoub, *The Qur'ān and Its Interpreters* (Albany, N.Y.: State University of New York Press, 1984), 1:8-11.

[7] Labib as-Said, *The Recited Koran* (Princeton, N.J.: The Darwin Press, 1975).

[8] David J. Goa, Harold G. Coward, Ronald Neufeldt, "Hindus in Alberta: Continuity and Change," *Canadian Ethnic Studies* 16 (1984), 103. Whereas traditional chanting of sacred scripture in India depended upon long periods of memorization and repetition in early childhood—a practice not likely to occur in Canada or even in modernized families in India—the guru mantra, it is claimed, requires no training in childhood for it to function in later life. It is said to fulfill the same spiritual role of keeping the mind controlled and focused on the Divine. Since the guru is merely a channel to the Divine, the mantra he or she gives is the psychological device for opening that channel and keeping it open. In traditional Hinduism this function was often fulfilled by the ritual learning and chanting of scripture.

[9] Goa and Coward, "Sacred Ritual, Sacred Language," 376.

[10] Jacques Ellul, *The Humiliation of the Word*, trans. Joyce Main Hanks (Grand Rapids, Mich.: Eerdmans Publishing Company, 1985), 1-4.

[11] Willem Jan Kooiman, *Luther and the Bible*, trans. John Schmidt (Philadelphia: Muhlenberg Press, 1961), 52.

[12] Ronald Bond, "The 'Lively Word' and the Book of Homilies: The Preaching and Reading Ministries in Tudor and Stuart England."

[13] See, for example, the dialogue between Indra (student) and Prajapati (the guru) regarding the real self in the Chāndogya Upaniṣad 8:7–8:12.

[14] T. R. V. Murti, *The Central Philosophy of Buddhism* (London: Allen and Unwin, 1960), chaps. 5-8.

[15] Heinrich Dumoulin, *A History of Zen Buddhism*, trans. Paul Peachey (New York: Pantheon Books, 1963), 130.

[16] Ibid., 133.

[17] Walter J. Ong, *Orality and Literacy: The Technologizing of the Word* (New York: Methuen, 1982), 8-9, 14-15.

[18] "Bibliolatry," *Encyclopedia of Religion and Ethics*, 3 vols., ed. James Hastings (New York: Scribner's, 1967).

[19] G. van der Leeuw, *Religion in Essence and Manifestation*, trans. J. E. Turner with additions by Hans Penner (New York: Harper & Row, 1963), 435-36.

1

Judaism

Eliezer Segal

Judaism is the religious way of life of the nation that has been known variously as Israel, the Hebrews, or the Jews. Though their homeland is in the Middle East, Jews are found throughout the world, and Judaism has taken diverse forms in its long history and geographic dispersion. Nevertheless, it has remained throughout a monotheistic faith, devoted to the unique all-powerful God who rules over nature and history. Jews see themselves as the descendants of the patriarch Abraham, who lived four thousand years ago and who entered into a covenant with God. Central to the covenant was adherence to a divinely revealed set of commandments and laws.

This chapter will describe the sacred scriptures of the Jews, as well as other texts and traditions that they hold as authoritative.

HILLEL AND THE TWO TORAHS

The following legend is told about the Jewish sage Hillel the Elder (first century B.C.E.). The ostensible subject of the interchange is the Torah, which (as we shall see in greater detail below) is the holiest section of the Jewish scriptures.

> A man once approached Hillel, and said to him: "Master, how many Torahs have been given?"
> [Hillel] replied to him: "Two: a written Torah and an oral Torah."
> [The man] said to him: "I trust you with regard to the written one, but not with regard to the oral one."
> [Hillel] said to him: "Sit down, my son." He then wrote him the *aleph bet* [the letters of the Hebrew alphabet].
> [Hillel] asked him: "What is this letter?"
> [The man] replied "*Aleph.*"
> He said: "It is not an *aleph* but a *bet.*"
> [Hillel] asked him: "What is this letter?"
> He said: "*Bet.*"
> [Hillel] said: "It is not a *bet* but a *gimel.*"
> [Hillel] said to him: "From where do you know that this is an *aleph* and this is a *bet* and this is a *gimel*? Indeed, thus has it been handed down from our ancestors that this is an *aleph* and this is a *bet* and this is a *gimel.* Just as you have accepted that on faith, so must you now accept this on faith."

This anecdote illustrates succinctly how, from early times, Jewish sages have been aware that the written text of the Torah cannot speak to us unless it is mediated through a living tradition. Ultimately, it is the unwritten tradition that chooses which books are to be accepted as authoritative, and assigns meaning and grammar to the graphic signs that make up the written language.

A TALE OF TWO FESTIVALS

The interplay between the written and oral facets of the religious tradition can be aptly illustrated in the following descriptions of two holidays in the Jewish annual calendar.

Holiday #1

The first holiday is bound closely to the agricultural cycles of the Land of Israel and its observance appears to be restricted to that geographical setting. On an unspecified date (evidently a Sunday) at the beginning of the grain harvest, a sheaf of the first produce (apparently barley) is given to a priest to be brought to the sanctuary. The priest waves the sheaf, then burns a lamb on the altar of the central sanctuary. This cultic ritual, an acknowledgment of the divine source of the agricultural bounty, must be performed before the new grain crop is permitted to be used for general consumption.

From that day seven weeks are counted, totalling forty-nine days. On the fiftieth day, on whichever date that turns out (evidently also a Sunday), two leavened loaves are offered by the priests in the sanctuary, accompanied by elaborate animal offerings of lambs, bullocks, rams, and assorted libations. This day is treated as a festival in that no servile work is to be performed. In most other respects its direct impact seems to be limited to the precincts of the Temple and to the hereditary priesthood who officiate therein. Therefore, one can raise some grave questions about the relevance of the holy day to Jews who dwell outside their homeland, or at a time when there is no Temple standing in Jerusalem. The purpose of the ceremony is not explicitly defined in scripture, though it would appear to be another expression of gratitude for the grain harvest.

Holiday #2

Our second holiday has a precisely defined date, on the sixth day of the Hebrew month of Sivan, though it can occur on any day of the week. This date marks the anniversary of a central event in Israel's sacred history, arguably the most important milestone in that long and eventful saga: the day on which the almighty God, Creator of the heaven and earth, appeared publicly to the assembled people of Israel at a mountain in the Sinai wilderness to reveal to them his sacred message. This revelation was initially a spoken one, uttered in the Hebrew language, though it was written down with meticulous precision by Moses, the greatest of God's prophets. According to traditional Jewish belief, the document that resulted from this revelation was the *Torah* ("teaching," "instruction") comprising the first five volumes of the Hebrew Bible. Every word and letter, copied faithfully over the generations, is sacred.

The celebration of this holiday is not focused in the Temple but in the home and in the synagogue; the latter institution, whose name derives from a Greek word meaning "house of assembly" (equivalent to the Hebrew *beit k'neset*), is a gathering point for all segments of the populace, not merely the priests. In the synagogue, communal prayers are recited, some of which are common to the daily liturgical structures and some of which are unique to the themes of this holy day, "the season of the giving of our Torah," as it is designated in many of the prayers. As an expression of the festival joy, passages from the biblical book of Psalms[1] are intoned by the congregation. The dramatic passage from the Torah that describes the Theophany at Mount Sinai is chanted from a Torah scroll, followed by a reading from the prophet Ezekiel's mystical vision of God enthroned upon an angelic chariot, a passage that is regarded as thematically similar in its portrayal of intimate contact between the celestial and mortal realms. The biblical book of Ruth, a pastoral romance that tells of the ancestry of the Israelite royal family, is also read. A scholar well-versed in the tradition, known as a Rabbi, gets up to speak before the congregation, expounding on the scriptural readings, explaining them in the light of the interpretations of traditional commentators, and concluding the sermon with a spirited exhortation to the assembled worshipers to intensify their devotion to the study and observance of the Torah.

The festive atmosphere extends to the home as well. As is the case on most Jewish holy days, the sanctity of the occasion is expressed primarily by means of the restrictions that are placed on workaday activities, though these are not as severe as on the weekly sabbath. For example, cooking is permitted on a festival,[2] as is the carrying of burdens in a public thoroughfare, though neither of these activities would be allowed on a Saturday. The family gathers for ceremonial meals. The evening meal is inaugurated with the recitation of the *Kiddush* blessing, in which the day is sanctified over a cup of wine. References to the holiday's theme are inserted into the grace after every meal. Many communities have special culinary traditions associated with the holiday, such as eating dairy dishes or fashioning the bread into symbolic shapes.[3]

What is arguably the most extraordinary fact about our description of the two festivals is that they are, in reality, the very same festival, the day known in Hebrew as *Shavu'ot*, the Feast of Weeks.

In the first version we restricted ourselves to the information contained in the written text of the Torah (Lv 23:9-21), whereas the second account described the elaborate and meaningful religious observances that developed in the Jewish oral tradition.

At first blush it is impossible to believe that the two descriptions could possibly be of the same holiday. The second is not an elaboration of the first but seems to contradict it on several crucial points! Does the holiday have a fixed date or does it not? Can it fall only on Sundays, or on other days as well? Was it ordained to give thanks for the grain harvest or to commemorate the revelation at Sinai? The two descriptions seem utterly incompatible with one another.

So extreme is the contrast that a study of the development of the Jewish Feast of Weeks provides an excellent example of both the interaction between written and oral traditions and the impact they have on the living community.

PHARISEES, SADDUCEES, AND ANCESTRAL TRADITIONS

The earliest sources that make conscious mention of a Jewish oral tradition are connected to sectarian debates that arose in the last centuries before the common era. Documents from that time note that the affirmation of an extra-scriptural tradition was originally the ideology of one faction among the several that fragmented the Judaism of the time: the movement known as Pharisaism.

Long before this stage of history, the authority of the Hebrew Bible had taken solid root among all segments of the community. No one disputed the divine origin of the Torah or the authority of its laws. There was also a consensus that the kind of divine communication that is embodied in the ancient Hebrew scriptures had long since come to an end and that God's message to humans now could be discovered only through a reading of the inspired teachings of the prophets of old.

Where disagreement did exist was on the question of authority *outside* the text of the Bible. The party known as the Sadducees, which represented the values and interests of the established high priesthood, argued that the received scripture, whose administration had been assigned to the priestly dynasties, was the exclusive repository of sacred teachings. Any tradition for which a source could not be found in the written Torah must be regarded as a human invention that could not lay claim to religious sanction. This excluded from the compass of Judaism many cherished practices and beliefs that had taken firm hold among the common people, largely composed of rural peasantry. It also implied that extensive realms of human experience are religiously irrelevant because they are not mentioned explicitly in the Torah.

A very different outlook was taught by the Pharisees. They were reluctant to acknowledge that the all-knowing author of the Torah had excluded anything from the scope of its guidance. Many traditions, though not written in the Bible, could be observed in the living experience of the covenant community. The ancient historian Josephus Flavius speaks of the Pharisees as being renowned for their expertise in the Law (that is, the Torah) and in the "ancestral traditions."[4] Insofar as we are able to reconstruct the content of these ancestral traditions during the second Jewish Commonwealth, it appears that they consisted largely of customs that had been adopted by the populace, sometimes from Babylonian or Persian influences, but which had no explicit source in the Law of Moses.[5] When the Second Jerusalem Temple was destroyed by the Romans in 70 C.E., the flexible Pharisaic ideology, with its belief in a religion that permeated every area of human endeavor, was the only stream to survive. It now evolved into what is customarily designated Rabbinic Judaism (after the title Rabbi, which was used to address their religious leaders). More significantly, through painstaking scholarship into the deepest levels of textual interpretation they were able to uncover scriptural teachings that were not apparent at a cursory reading. Thus, the Rabbis cultivated a model of spiritual authority that was vested not in priestly pedigree or in withdrawal from the mainstream society, but in scholarship, devotion, and community involvement.

The ancient Rabbis bequeathed to us a rich literary record of their studies of the written and oral traditions. These were classified under the general categories of *Halakhah* (law) and *aggadah* (homiletics, exegesis, moral maxims, etc.). The most authoritative of these works was the legal compendium known as the *Mishnah,* completed in Palestine in the early third century; encyclopedic collections of discussions based on the Mishnah, known as Talmuds, were composed over the following centuries.[6] Throughout ancient times, a strict prohibition was maintained against putting those traditions into writing. Commentaries and law codes continue to be composed to this day.

There are several features about the evolution of the Feast of Weeks that can serve as instructive illustrations of the methods and objectives of the oral tradition in its interactions with the written scripture.

LUNAR AND SOLAR CALENDARS

Let us begin with that irreconcilable mystery of a festival that at once has an identifiable date on the calendar—and yet has none. This contradiction is rooted in the Hebrew wording of Leviticus (23:11), where the counting of the seven weeks is said to begin after the *shabbat*, the day of rest that is usually presumed to be Saturday. In this unique instance the sages of the oral Torah insisted that a different day was being identified, the first day of Passover (which was mentioned in the previous passage), when, as on all biblical festival days, work was prohibited. To the outsider, that interpretation appears utterly inconsistent with the standard usage.

From the Dead Sea Scrolls we now know that at issue was more than the interpretation of a single biblical passage or the celebration of a particular festival. The rival Jewish movements of the Second Commonwealth were stubbornly promoting radically different calendars. This was not a question of life rhythms or astronomical calculation but involved grave questions of sacred law. According to the Torah, the violation of festival prohibitions—working on a day of rest, eating on the Day of Atonement, or consuming leavened bread on Passover—incurred severe penalties, whether they were executed by human or supernatural agencies. A situation in which one segment of the community treated as profane what for others was holy made it impossible for those segments to dwell together.

Although the Bible dates events in months and years, we do not know exactly what it means by those concepts. Some postbiblical movements adhered to a sophisticated solar year totalling 364 days, a number that had the advantage of being evenly divisible by seven. This meant that holidays could also be counted on to recur on the same day of the week in every subsequent year. Therefore, for adherents of this calendar, such as the authors of many of the Dead Sea Scrolls, it was crucial that the Feast of Weeks be identified by its place in the week rather than the month.[7]

The accepted Jewish calendar, championed by the common people and their Pharisaic representatives, is composed of months that are measured according to the actual phases of the moon, that is, months of twenty-nine or thirty days. Since twelve such months add up to only 354 days, an additional thirteenth month is appended to certain years in order to restore synchronization with the solar cycles that determine the agricultural seasons, and hence are crucial to the themes of many of the Jewish festivals.

The historian might be inclined to view the Jewish adoption of this reckoning as a simple borrowing from the Babylonian or Metonic systems. However, there is much more at stake. Built into the foundations of this lunar-solar calendar, as it was implemented by Rabbinic Judaism, is the need for the community itself to decide when every month begins and when to insert the extra months. The sages of the oral tradition saw it as a profound act of partnership between the divine and mortal realms. In a bold Rabbinic homily we hear of God consenting to postpone the judgment of humanity, which normally takes place on the Hebrew New Year, until his human children have officially announced the determination of the beginning of the month.

> If, for any reason, the court decides to put off the beginning of the year by one day, the Holy One tells the ministering angels: "Remove the dais, dismiss the advocates, dismiss the clerks, since the court on earth has decreed that the New Year will not begin till tomorrow."[8]

MIDRASH: THE ORAL TRADITION INTERPRETS THE WRITTEN

As always, the evolution of the oral tradition was tied to the meticulous examination of the written text. The Hebrew term for this activity is *Midrash* ("seeking out"). Historians have suggested that many of the distinctive midrashic tropes were borrowed from the modes of Greek and Latin rhetoric and legal discourse;[9] however, the genre is quintessentially Jewish, founded upon the belief in the divine authorship of the scriptures. Because every letter and calligraphic ornamentation in the Bible is believed to be of infinite significance, it is therefore a religious duty to uncover as much as possible of its many layers of meaning.[10] Toward that end they cultivated sophisticated methods of eliciting from the text far more than is visible to the casual reader.

In our present instance, we can appreciate how carefully the Rabbis traced the Torah's time line of the Israelites' sojourn in the wilderness from their departure from Egypt on Passover until their encampment beneath Mount Sinai.[11] They noted that only by assuming the validity of the traditional lunar-solar calendar could they arrive at the correspondence between the dates of the scriptural Feast of Weeks and of the most important anniversary in Jewish sacred history, the revelation of the Torah itself. Without this, Judaism would be left without any ritual day of commemoration for this occasion.

SCRIPTURE IN THE SYNAGOGUE

Another conspicuous feature in the living celebration of the Feast of Weeks was its celebration in the synagogue. This is another institution whose origins are unclear to the historians, but which has exercised a decisive influence on Jewish spirituality from the beginnings of the common era. Some trace it to the Babylonian captivity, where it served as a center of communal religious expression for generations who had been deprived of their holy Temple. Others see its beginnings in the attempts of Egyptian Jews in the third century B.C.E. to overcome their geographic separation from Jerusalem. At any rate, the synagogue came to coexist with the Jerusalem sanctuary, allowing expression to religious needs that could not be accommodated by the priestly sacrificial service.[12]

Although the synagogue later came to be identified with the recitation of formal communal prayer, a form of devotional worship that was not prescribed in the scriptural tradition, the earliest records associate it with the reading and teaching of the Torah.

The five volumes of the Torah constitute the core of the Jewish sacred scriptures. They are believed to be entirely of divine origin, with no significant human component. However, Jews recognize a larger body of ancient literature as being *prophetic,* that is, issuing from divine revelation or inspiration. The Jewish Bible contains the same works that are found in the standard Christian "Old Testament" (twenty-four books according to the traditional division).[13]

The prevailing Jewish classification divides the Hebrew Bible into three sections:

Torah: Relating the history of Israel from the creation until the death of the prophet Moses. Central to the Torah is the large body of laws and precepts revealed through Moses at Mount Sinai.

Prophets: Historical narratives tracing the history of the nation until the beginnings of the Second Commonwealth; as well as the teachings of "prophets," spiritual figures who arose to proclaim God's word to the people.

Sacred Writings (often designated in the Greek form, "Hagiographa"): a heterogeneous assortment of texts, mostly from the later years of the biblical era.[14]

Although the traditional Jewish belief is that the full text of the Torah was revealed directly to Moses, historical scholarship sees it as a composite work that evolved over many generations out of diverse documents and oral traditions, reaching its definitive form during the era of the Babylonian captivity (ca. 587-30 B.C.E.). biblical tradition itself (Neh 8) relates how the Torah of Moses was publicly read in Jerusalem before the full assembly of the returned exiles, who took it upon themselves to conduct their private and communal lives in accordance with its precepts. Because Jewish tradition has always insisted that members of the community be intimately familiar with the sacred laws contained in holy scripture, religious study and education have always been supreme values.

The Hebrew term that is employed in ancient Jewish texts to designate the full Jewish Bible is *Miqra'*, which means "recitation from a written text." This reflects its standing in the liturgical rhythm of the community. Public assemblies are convened on regular occasions during which the texts from the Bible are read aloud to the people, as the Torah had been read by Ezra. In large measure the structures that were set in place for this purpose in ancient times are still operative today.

The main lectionary cycle is for the sequential reading of the Torah on Saturdays, the biblical Sabbath. Consecutive sections are read each week until the five books have been completed. In the ancient Palestinian rite the readings were distributed so that they could be completed in about three and a half years. Currently, almost all Jewish communities follow the Babylonian practice of completing the reading of the Torah over a single year.

The Torah is also read publicly on festivals and other special calendar events. For those occasions a passage is selected that relates to the theme of the day. According to a longstanding practice, readings are also ordained for Saturday afternoon, as well as Monday and Thursday mornings. In this way no Jew would have to go more than three days without exposure to the words of Torah.[15] The weekday readings are very brief, consisting of the first few verses of the larger section that will be read on the following Saturday morning.

The ritual reading must be done from a handwritten scroll inscribed on parchment according to precise regulations. Each copy must be letter-perfect; if an error or erasure should be discovered, then the scroll must be removed from use until it is corrected. In this way the precise text of the Bible has been preserved with remarkable accuracy for thousands of years.

The Hebrew alphabet in which biblical texts are written does not have visual signs for most vowels. Furthermore, there is a traditional system of cantillation that incorporates both syntactic and musical elements for chanting the biblical texts in the synagogue. Initially, all these features could be transmitted only through memorization, a demanding process that occupied the main portion of the elementary school curriculum.[16] Even though a system of written notation for the vowels and musical chanting was introduced in the early medieval era, these signs may not be written into the scrolls that are read in the synagogue, so that the ability to read the Bible in the synagogue requires extensive skill and effort.

In the liturgical reading of the Torah the passages are apportioned among several individuals,[17] in proportion to the sanctity of the day, ranging from three on a weekday to seven on the Sabbath. Though originally these participants performed the actual reading, it is now normal, since so few individuals are competent to read from an unvocalized text, to have a trained functionary do the reading, while the participants recite blessings at the opening and conclusion of the designated portions.[18]

An ancient liturgical practice that has fallen into disuse is that of providing a translation (Targum) after each verse in Aramaic, the language spoken by most Jews in Israel and Babylonia. With the decline of Aramaic, the spoken Targum has been abandoned by almost all Jewish communities, though the ancient Aramaic versions are still studied.[19]

The sacred scrolls of the Torah are the focal point of a synagogue. They are clothed in decorative casings or mantles, which are often based on regal imagery, and housed in a special "ark" in the front of the sanctuary. Their removal for reading or their return to the ark is done in solemn procession as worshipers symbolically kiss them in adoration. At the conclusion of a public reading they are raised aloft and the congregation recites "and this is the law that Moses placed before the Children of Israel" (Dt 4:44). Out of respect, the congregation remains standing at any time the Torah is not at rest in the closed ark or on its reading table.

On Sabbaths and festivals the reading from the Torah is concluded with a passage from the Prophets. The passage is usually selected based on a thematic affinity to the reading in the Torah, though the connection is sometimes related to other calendric considerations. Most of the Hagiographa books are not read formally in the synagogue, the exceptions being five scrolls that are associated with certain annual holy days.

Analogous to the phenomenon of *translating* the Bible for the community was the very ancient practice of *expounding* it, that is, of creatively interpreting the biblical text in order to make it relevant to the needs and concerns of the living congregation. The synagogue sermon, usually delivered on Sabbaths and festivals, developed into a very sophisticated rhetorical form, incorporating scholarship, spiritual sensitivity, and literary virtuosity.[20]

TORAH IN DAILY LIFE

For all the import of the synagogue in Jewish religious life, it remains only one setting among many for the expression of Jewish spirituality.[21] The comprehensive scope of Torah law embraces aspects of life that liberal society would not regard as religious, including the food one eats, sexual conduct, the garments one wears, laws of torts and contract, and much more.

Though many of its laws ostensibly deal with the same issues that we would now expect to find in the civil and criminal codes of secular states, the belief that they were commanded by a divine legislator transforms them into religious categories. Among contemporary Jewish thinkers, Rabbi J. D. Soleveitchik stated most cogently how the all-encompassing categories of the Jewish Law (Halakhah) impose a metaphysical structure upon physical existence:

> Halakhah has a fixed a priori relationship to the whole of reality in all of its fine and detailed particulars. Halakhic

> man orients himself to the entire cosmos and tries to understand it by utilizing an ideal world which he bears in his halakhic consciousness. All halakhic concepts are a priori, and it is through them that halakhic man looks at the world.[22]

In our description of the *Shavu'ot* meal we noted how it is embedded in a framework of prayers and blessings. The evolution of these liturgical practices provides additional models of the interweaving of the written and oral traditions.

Thus, the written Torah commands that "You shall eat and be full, and you shall bless the Lord your God" (Dt 8:10). The oral tradition formulated the specific blessings to be uttered upon the consumption of particular foodstuffs (designating separate blessings for bread, fruits of the tree, fruits of the earth, etc.), in order to express gratitude for every God-given benefit and pleasure.[23]

The Torah contains repeated injunctions to observe a weekly day of rest, as well as to refrain from labor on festival days; however, only a few specific activities fall under the heading of "forbidden work." The oral tradition (as recorded in the Mishnah) carefully enumerated thirty-nine principal categories of forbidden labor, from which are derived many particular actions. The Rabbis have also added preventative prohibitions in order to further prevent transgressions of the Torah's commands. Through history the nature of the Sabbath has changed in response to the changing conditions of life. Thus, for most observant Jews in the contemporary world the keeping of the Sabbath is often most immediately felt in their refraining from the use of electricity or telephones, activities that were not explicitly discussed in any of the ancient texts.[24]

Similarly, a vague biblical injunction to "remember the Sabbath day to keep it holy" (Ex 20:9) was transformed by the sages of the oral tradition into the ceremony of *Kiddush*, a special blessing that is pronounced over a cup of wine on the onset of a holy day. A parallel ritual, the *Havdalah* is recited at the conclusion of a Sabbath or festival to mark the separation between the holy and the profane.[25]

The preparation and consumption of the food are also transformed into a religious act, irrespective of the festival context. The Torah's fragmentary regulations defining permitted and prohibited species, bans against creatures that died of disease or "seething a kid in its mother's milk," and the need to designate portions of produce for the upkeep of the priests, poor and others, were expanded in the oral tradition into an intricate dietary regimen. Observant Jews must therefore be ever conscious of the ingredients that enter their bodies, whether there is any admixture of dairy and meat items, how meat was slaughtered, and much more.[26]

INTERPRETING THE COMMANDMENTS

These laws serve many purposes in the lives of committed Jews. In addition to being expressions of their readiness to obey God's commands, they also accustom Jews to a pattern of disciplined self-restraint. Because the rules of kosher food preparation extend to the utensils and the ovens, it is virtually impossible for Jews who observe these rules to eat in restaurants or in the homes of non-Jews, a fact that was recognized by the ancient sages as reinforcing Jewish distinctiveness and the integrity of the family.

A straightforward reading of the Torah quickly demonstrates that God's unique revelation was not intended to convey a systematic theology or a guide to mystical experience of the Divine; nor does it provide clear visions of the afterlife or of the climax of history. First and foremost, the Torah is a book of laws, or, to capture its religious significance, it is a collection of *commandments*. Central to the religion of the Bible is the conviction that, in their observance of the commandments of the Torah, the people of Israel are fulfilling their obligations in a national religious covenant with God that defines their spiritual vocation.

Jewish thinkers over the ages would grapple with the question of the reasons for the commandments. Some would insist that the quest for their rationale implies an unacceptable rejection of their absolute authority as the word of God, while promoting the arrogant human delusion that we are capable of comprehending the divine mind.[27] Others took the opposite position, that to refrain from understanding the reasons for the commandments would foster the image of a God who is arbitrary or irrational, whose Torah is out of tune with the human situation.[28] Most would take intermediary positions, acknowledging that some biblical precepts have manifestly ethical and utilitarian reasons, whereas others (especially those related to areas like purity and sacrificial worship) are plainly beyond our comprehension; and many are susceptible to multiple interpretations.

Thus Maimonides observed that the counting of days between Passover and *Shavu'ot* teaches in easily understandable terms how the political liberty achieved by the Egyptian Exodus was only a means toward the ultimate spiritual perfection that is embodied in the Sinai revelation.[29] On the other hand, the mystical classic the *Zohar* depicts it as a purification from metaphysical evil and analogous to the eager anticipation of an ecstatic union between husband and wife following a prolonged separation.[30]

ETERNALLY NEW

Later scholars would pose questions: Why did the Torah insist on being so cryptic in disguising the date of "the season of the giving of our Torah"? Why did it not treat the Feast of Weeks like Passover, for instance, whose date on the fifteenth day of the first month is plainly linked to the time of Israel's Exodus from Egyptian slavery?

An incisive answer was offered by the famous Polish Jewish preacher Rabbi Solomon Ephraim Luntshitz (d. 1619) in his *K'li Yaqar* commentary to Leviticus 23:26. In a statement that summarizes exquisitely the value of oral tradition in maintaining the Torah's dynamic vitality for the people of Israel, he wrote:

> This is so because the Torah must remain as new for each person every day as it was on that day when it was received from Mount Sinai. For the Lord chose not to define a specific date, since *on each and every day* of the year it

should appear to us as if on that day we received it from Mount Sinai.

Suggested Reading

Aminoah, Noah, and Yosef Nitzan. n.d. *Torah: The Oral Tradition.* Translated by Haim Schachter and Larry Moscovitz. [Jerusalem]: World Zionist Organization Department for Torah Education and Culture in the Diaspora.
Heschel, Abraham Joshua. 1966. *The Earth Is the Lord's, and the Sabbath.* Harper Torchbooks ed. New York: Harper & Row.
Jacobs, Louis. 1984. *A Tree of Life: Diversity, Flexibility, and Creativity in Jewish Law.* New York: Oxford University Press.
Steinsaltz, Adin. 1976. *The Essential Talmud.* New York: Basic Books.
Trepp, Leo. 1980. *The Complete Book of Jewish Observance.* New York: Summit Books.

Notes

[1] Psalms 113-18, recited on festive occasions as the *Hallel* ("Praise").

[2] The tradition evolved its detailed regulations based on Exodus 12:16.

[3] Isaac Klein, *A Guide to Jewish Religious Practice*, Moreshet series, vol. 6 (New York: Jewish Theological Seminary of America/dist. by Klav Pub. House, 1979), 147-52.

[4] Josephus, *Jewish Antiquities*, 13:10:6 (297-98). Cf. Mk 7:3ff.; Mt 15:2ff.; Acts 22:3; Gal 1:14.

[5] Shaye J. D. Cohen, *From the Maccabees to the Mishnah,* 1st ed,, Library of Early Christianity, vol. 7 (Philadelphia: Westminster, 1987), esp. 146-64.

[6] An excellent guide to this literature is Hermann Leberecht Strack, Günter Stemberger, and Markus N. A. Bockmuehl, *Introduction to the Talmud and Midrash* (Edinburgh: T. & T. Clark, 1991).

[7] Shemaryahu Talmon, *The World of Qumran from Within: Collected Studies* (Jerusalem: Magnes Press, 1989).

[8] See *Pesikta de-Rab Kahana: R. Kahana's Compilation of Discourses for Sabbaths and Festal Days*, trans. William G. Braude, and Israel J. Kapstein (Philadelphia: Jewish Publication Society of America, 1976), 115 (5:13).

[9] Saul Lieberman, *Hellenism in Jewish Palestine: Studies in the Literary Transmission, Beliefs and Manners of Palestine in the 1st Century B.C.E.–4th Century C.E.* (New York: The Jewish Theological Semi-

nary of America, 1962), 65-67; David Daube, "Rabbinic Methods of Interpretation and Hellenistic Rhetoric," *Hebrew Union College Annual* 22 (1949): 239–65.

[10] Eliezer Segal, "Midrash and Literature: Some Medieval Views," *Prooftexts* 11 (1991): 57-65.

[11] The calculations are set out in the Babylonian Talmud *Shabbat* 86b-88a.

[12] Cohen, *From the Maccabees to the Mishnah*, 111-15.

[13] The apparent divergence from the number of books in standard English Bibles is the result of different conventions of grouping them.

[14] See Cohen, *From the Maccabees to the Mishnah,* 182-95. The differentiation between the Prophets and Hagiographa does not seem to be a qualitative one so much as a chronological sequence, in that a recognized corpus of "prophetic writings" was already in existence before it was supplemented by the works in the third section.

[15] See Babylonian Talmud *Baba Qamma* 82a.

[16] S. D. Goitein, *A Mediterranean Society: The Jewish Communities of the Arab World as Portrayed in the Documents of the Cairo Genizah* (Berkeley and Los Angeles: University of California Press, 1967), 2:174-75. This is the original significance of the rabbinic proverb, "The world exists solely through the breath of the schoolchildren," that is, through their memorizing the correct reading of the Bible.

[17] According to traditionalist practice, these must be adult male Jews.

[18] Klein, *A Guide to Jewish Religious Practice,* 27-33.

[19] Cohen, *From the Maccabees to the Mishnah,* 210-11.

[20] Joseph Heinemann and Jakob Josef Petuchowski, *Literature of the Synagogue*, Library of Jewish Studies (New York: Behrman House, 1975).

[21] Non-Jews often treat *synagogue* as the Jewish equivalent of *church,* but this is misleading. The word "synagogue" refers only to a building with a defined function; it is never equated with the entirety of Judaism in the way that "the church" is identified with the manifestations of Christianity in the world.

[22] Joseph Dov Soloveitchik, *Halakhic Man*, 1st Eng. ed. (Philadelphia: Jewish Publication Society of America, 1983), 23.

[23] Klein, *A Guide to Jewish Religious Practice,* 41-49.

[24] Ibid., 78-94.

[25] Ibid., 61-62, 73-75.

[26] Ibid., 302-78. In our contemporary world, where much of our food comes to us from the supermarket shelves, this alertness frequently takes the form of careful reading of certifications on the package.

[27] Ephraim E. Urbach, *The Sages: The Concepts and Beliefs*, trans. I. Abrams (Jerusalem: Magues Press, 1979), 1:365-99.

[28] Thus according to the foremost medieval Jewish philosopher Moses Maimonides, in his *Guide of the Perplexed*, trans. with intro. and notes by Shlomo Pines (Chicago: University of Chicago Press, 1963), 3:31 (523-24).

[29] Ibid., 3:34.

[30] See Eliezer Segal, "The Exegetical Craft of the *Zohar*: Towards an Appreciation," *AJS Review* 17, no. 1 (1992): 31-49, 40-47.

2

The Nature and Function of Oral and Written Scripture for the Christian Devotee

Wayne O. McCready

SCRIPTURE AND CHRISTIANITY—AN INTRODUCTION

The working context of this chapter on Christianity is that the term *scripture*—in its oral and written forms—captures the essence of how sacred word and sacred text function in this religion both at the corporate level of formal expression and at the experiential level of the devotee. That is, the English word *scripture*, with its Latin (*scriptura*, "writing"), Greek (*graphè*, "writing, letter, inscription"), and Hebrew (*ketāb*, "writing") etymological influences, underscores the primacy of central written texts in a closed canon. This particular feature of Christianity need not apply in other religious traditions in which central written texts may not be as important or easily identifiable; the oral and aural ("received through hearing") dimensions of scripture may be more fundamental than written texts. Thus scholars prefer the term *sacred word and sacred text* when working in a religiously pluralistic environment because it does not predetermine whether written texts are more important than speaking or hearing scripture. This study will seek to balance multireligious considerations while affirming that for Christianity a book-orientation is the first principle for understanding sacred word and sacred text in this religion (the Greek term *byblos*, "book," in second to fourth century C.E. Christianity referred to the Old and New Testaments; the Latin term *biblia* is the root-word for Bible). The primacy of a textual orientation, however, does not minimize the oral and aural features of scripture in Christianity. Indeed, as we shall see below, Christian texts that became authoritative and influential in the first two centuries of the common era emerged from oral contexts; also, they were written with the intention of being read aloud and heard by Christian audiences in the early church. This chapter will outline essential factors about the nature and function of Christian scripture in oral and written settings, with emphasis on formative stages of the religion, and will comment on how scripture is experienced by the devotee.

FEATURES OF SCRIPTURE

Before moving to specific considerations of scripture in Christianity, it is worthwhile to outline five features about sacred word and sacred text from a multireligious perspective. Scholars working in specific religions, but with an eye toward holistic assessments of scripture from a global perspective, typically cite these features to provide context on the character of sacred word and sacred text in a particular religion, and also to reflect on how scriptures in various religions demonstrate similarities and differences.[1] These features serve as part of the basis for dealing with scripture in this study of Christianity.

- scripture is a generic entity reflecting a common kind of religious orientation, even though specifics of scripture vary in form and content among religions; this generic entity typically addresses questions such as Why am I here?, Where am I going?, and What is life about?;
- scripture refers to what is especially sacred and especially authoritative, because it deals with matters of ultimate concern and it functions as the basis of appeal for practice and belief;

- scripture is not represented by any one fixed form; one cannot open a book and determine that it is scripture by its literary form and content;
- scripture is fundamentally relational; what is especially sacred and especially authoritative is so, insofar as practitioners and believers of a religion perceive it as sacred and authoritative; a religious community affirms that scripture deals with matters of ultimate concern in a manner that is somehow unique, and thus it is distinguished from other forms of speech and writing; this relational feature highlights the interactive dynamic between scripture and religious communities, that is, communities shape and receive scripture/scripture shapes and creates religious communities;
- scripture involves written and oral/aural (what is received through hearing) dimensions and there is an interdependency (an interpenetration) between these two aspects of scripture; scriptures are not only written, translated, copied, preserved and displayed, but they are also sung, chanted, read aloud, memorized, and retold; these dimensions call attention to the functional dynamic that exists between religious communities and their scriptures.

The magnitude of sacred text and sacred word over the course of human history is such that researchers conclude that humans are inclined to scripturalize. That is, humans regularly promote sayings, poetry, wisdom stories, historical narratives, magic, songs, legends, moral philosophy, sermons, ethical recommendations—and other forms of speech and literature—as especially sacred and especially authoritative. Wilfred Cantwell Smith writes:

> One way and another, scripture has played a major role in human history, not only in individual and corporate piety and moral sensibility and intellectual vision, but in law, family relations, literature, art, economic patterns, social and political organization, social and political revolutions, dress, linguistic usage, and otherwise.[2]

Scripturalizing as a human propensity and human activity involves not only determining and promoting what is understood to be especially sacred and especially authoritative—it is a consequence of people engaging with issues of ultimate concern and hence provides access to what it means to be human. With reference to how the word is experienced in the life of a devotee, the proposal that humans are inclined to scripturalize suggests that it is not only a religio-historical matter but an ongoing activity in contemporary society.

SCRIPTURE, ORIGINS OF CHRISTIANITY AND ITS DEVELOPMENT

Origins of Christianity

Scholarly assessments on the beginnings of Christianity suggest that it started as a religious renewal group in Second Temple Judaism during the mid-first century of the common era. On matters of religion, Second Temple Judaism was characterized by three principles: (1) belief in monotheism (the Jewish God); (2) belief that God was to be worshiped through offering sacrifices, with the majority of Jews doing so at a magnificent Temple in Jerusalem; and (3) belief that God revealed expectations for humans in texts considered especially sacred and especially authoritative. These texts were sometimes referred to as Torah ("guide, directive, law"). The primary religious authorities were Jerusalem priests, who officiated at the sacrifices offered in the Jerusalem Temple with religious renewal groups (e.g., Pharisees, Sadducees, Essenes, Qumranites, and the Jesus movement) functioning as a counter-balancing influence in society by promoting various practices and interpretations having to do with how humans encountered God, matters about sacrificial worship, and what was involved in responding to the content of Torah. Renewal groups numbered about fifteen thousand out of a total population in the Jewish homeland of some one million in the first century C.E. Jesus of Nazareth, the founding figure of the religion that eventually was called Christianity, was a first-century Jew. His immediate followers were Jews who believed that Jesus, as a religious-renewal figure, established an era radically different from those prior. They spoke of a new relationship with

God (a new covenant); a new community, the people of God (new creatures in Christ); and a new age for humans (the kingdom of God). These were based on their belief that Jesus was Christ (literally, "anointed one," but in Christianity it distinguished Jesus' relationship of Son to Father).[3] In the first century of the beginnings of Christianity (ca. 30-150 C.E.) its membership changed from being primarily Jewish to being predominantly Gentile (that is, not Jewish) as a result of active missionizing in the larger Mediterranean world.

The Old Testament

Jesus' followers, like other religious renewal groups in the first century C.E., embraced religious texts that they viewed as sacred; indeed, their profile in society as a renewal group was largely determined by particular interpretations of sacred texts. The discovery of the Dead Sea Scrolls in 1947 clearly demonstrated that the range, content, and literary forms of texts viewed as especially sacred and especially authoritative among first century C.E. Jews were vast and varied.[4] Also, Jews in the first century C.E. read and spoke a variety of languages, with the consequence that Jewish scriptures were available in a number of editions and translations including Hebrew, Greek, Aramaic, and Syriac. Because early Christians successfully missionized among Gentiles who spoke and read Greek, the Jewish scriptures used by the majority of Christians were based on a Greek version called the Septuagint or the "Old Testament" (2 Corinthians 3:6-14 refers to reading an "old covenant/testament" that stands in contrast to the "new covenant/testament" of Christianity). The arrangement and content of the Christian Old Testament listed below reflect variations among Catholic, Orthodox, and Protestant editions in traditional thematic groupings of texts. In the sixteenth century, Protestant reformers reduced the number of texts in their version of the Old Testament from forty-six to thirty-nine books to parallel those found in the Hebrew Bible, although they kept the traditional Christian numbering (e.g., 1 and 2 Samuel rather than one book, Shemuel, as in the Hebrew Bible) and arrangement; typically, Protestant Bibles refer to the additional seven books as apocrypha or deuterocanonical ("second canon") books.

The Christian Old Testament

	Roman Catholic and Orthodox	Protestant
Pentateuch	1. Genesis	1. Genesis
	2. Exodus	2. Exodus
	3. Leviticus	3. Leviticus
	4. Numbers	4. Numbers
	5. Deuteronomy	5. Deuteronomy
Historical Books	6. Joshua	6. Joshua
	7. Judges	7. Judges
	8. Ruth	8. Ruth
	9-10. 1 & 2 Samuel	9-10. 1 & 2 Samuel
	11-12. 1 & 2 Kings	11-12. 1 & 2 Kings
	13-14. 1 & 2 Chronicles	13-14. 1 & 2 Chronicles
	15-16. Ezra & Nehemiah	15-16. Ezra & Nehemiah
	17. Tobit	Deuterocanonical
	18. Judith	Deuterocanonical
	19. Esther*	17. Esther
Poetry and Wisdom	20. Job	18. Job
	21. Psalms	19. Psalms
	22. Proverbs	20. Proverbs
	23. Ecclesiastes	21. Ecclesiastes
	24. Song of Solomon	22. Song of Solomon
	25. Wisdom of Solomon	Deuterocanonical
	26. Ecclesiasticus (Wisdom of Ben Sira)	Deuterocanonical
Prophets	27. Isaiah	23. Isaiah
	28. Jeremiah	24. Jeremiah
	29. Lamentations of Jeremiah	25. Lamentations
	30. Baruch**	Deuterocanonical
	31. Ezekiel	26. Ezekiel
	32. Daniel*	27. Daniel

* Roman Catholic versions of Esther and Daniel are larger than Orthodox and Protestant versions; in deuterocanonical listings they include The Story of Susanna, The Song of the Three Children, and The Story of Bel and the Dragon. The Prayer of Manasseh is not part of the Roman Catholic Old Testament canon but frequently is listed among deuterocanonical texts.

** The Roman Catholic version of Baruch includes the Letter of Jeremiah as chapter 6 in the Book of Baruch; in other versions of the Old Testament it usually is listed with deuterocanonical books.

33. Hosea	28. Hosea
34. Joel	29. Joel
35. Amos	30. Amos
36. Obadiah	31. Obadiah
37. Jonah	32. Jonah
38. Micah	33. Micah
39. Nahum	34. Nahum
40. Habakkuk	35. Habakkuk
41. Zephaniah	36. Zephaniah
42. Haggai	37. Haggai
43. Zechariah	38. Zechariah
44. Malachi	39. Malachi
45-46 1 & 2 Maccabees	Deuterocanonical

The Old Testament and the Christian Devotee

A number of observations about the Christian Old Testament can be drawn from these lists. First, the English translations followed Latin editions, which were translations of Greek texts. Greek versions of Jewish scriptures were translations of earlier Hebrew texts (or in limited cases Aramaic, as in Daniel 2:4-7:28). There is not a primacy of sacred language for Christian scriptures, and thus a devotee need not learn languages of the first manuscripts, such as Greek or Hebrew, to engage with the texts in a meaningful way. Rather, the emphasis is on translating scripture into the vernacular (the term Vulgate usually refers to the official Latin version of the Bible for Western Christianity, but it means "popular, common," as in the vernacular or common speech).

Even though Christianity promoted a canon of scripture (Greek *kanōn,* "rule, guide") by the fourth century, with specific and designated texts held to be especially sacred and especially authoritative, the Old Testament is not fixed. As we saw above, the canon of the Old Testament for Roman Catholic and Orthodox Christian communities differs from the canon of the Old Testament of Protestants; there are also differences between Roman Catholic and Orthodox editions. Important figures from all camps in Christianity have held a variety of opinions on the canonical status of certain books in the Old Testament. The point here is not about divisiveness but rather that the Old Testament affirms a basic principle about scripture: it is not a fixed entity. Decisions on its form and content were made by communities of faith on issues of practice and belief set in historically specific contexts, and they underscore the relational dynamic of scripture. The denominations in Christianity shaped received scriptures by placing them in a canon and giving them that particular status; the received scriptures shaped and influenced communities of Christians because they served as a primary resource for defining denominational practices and theologies.

A common assessment of the Old Testament portion of the Christian Bible is that it represents a distinctive feature of this religion. That is, one finds sacred texts of one religion, Judaism, embraced by another religion, Christianity. This is as much wrong as it is right. Normative Judaism, that is Rabbinic Judaism, from the first century C.E. to the modern period, draws on scriptures from Second Temple Judaism (ca. 450 B.C.E.–150 C.E.), the Israelite religion (ca. 1000–450 B.C.E.) and the Hebrew religion (ca. 1500–1000 B.C.E.). So does Christianity. The beginnings of Rabbinic Judaism and the origins of Christianity are as twins born from the same womb, with each sibling going its own direction as it gained unique and distinctive characteristics.[5] Rabbinic Judaism and traditional Christianity are heirs to the same scriptural inheritance. Over its first two centuries, Christianity gradually moved outside of the widest definition of being Jewish and charted its own course as a separate world religion.

The significance of this common inheritance of scripture is threefold. First, an important portion of Christian scriptures (that is, the Old Testament) are Jewish scriptures in origin, and as a consequence, Christian devotees inevitably deal with religious pluralism by the very nature of their scripture. Reviews on the Christian capacity to deal with this matter are mixed. As a religion of the majority in Western cultures, Christians frequently assumed that Christian interpretations of texts found in the Old Testament were not only self-evident but that they were the *only* interpretations. This resulted in persecution of Jews by Christians over the centuries, especially on issues relating to messianic expectations. Yet historically, Christianity affirmed and reaffirmed its Jewish origins (that is, religious pluralism as foundational) through texts viewed as especially sacred and especially authoritative by both world religions. This complex feature of Christianity is a source of vitality and creativity because Christians have been forced by the very nature of their scripture to look beyond their own boundaries when dealing with religious identity and definition.

Second, the unique character of Christianity was formed as a consequence of its engagement with Jewish scriptures about claims that Jesus was the messiah. Christians looked to the Old Testament on a number of important issues for religious practice and belief, but no topic rivaled the use of scripture as a source for understanding and articulating Christian messianism. While messianism was a Jewish idea having to do with leadership through kings and priests, Christianity, through its reading and interpretation of Old Testament texts, particularized it and to a large degree molded the concept in its own religious image by proclaiming that Jesus was the messiah (the Greek term for messiah was *christos*, "christ") as Son to Father in his relationship to God. This proclamation was an important factor in moving Christianity outside of the widest definition of being Jewish and helped set the course for Christianity to gain its own distinctive character as a world religion. The religious texts inherited from its Jewish origins serve as a substantial and creative resource for Christian messianism, and it is this factor that historically has convinced Christians to read Jewish scriptures as especially sacred and especially authoritative.

Third, by receiving and affirming inherited scriptures from its birthplace in Second Temple Judaism, Christianity places particular significance on *texts* as central to its self-definition as a world religion. Without doubt, Old Testament texts have been read aloud, sung, told, and retold in a range of social, communal, and family settings. The oral and aural dimensions of the Old Testament complement its written counterpart; one cannot image Christianity being successful in its missionizing enterprises without the force and impact of oral and aural scripture. But at the end of the day, the primacy of Old Testament written texts functions as a basis for individual transformation and renewal, as an intellectual resource for doctrinal developments on a range of topics, and as a guide on matters of Christian orthodoxy when hard decisions are required as the religion deals with in-house issues of practices and belief.

THE NEW TESTAMENT AND THE ORIGINS OF CHRISTIANITY REVISITED

As previously mentioned, religious renewal groups in Second Temple Judaism—such as Pharisees, Sadducees, Essenes, Qumranites, and the Jesus movement—provided social and religious commentary on issues they judged to be important; an essential reference point for these groups was Jewish scriptures. Inherited scriptures (such as those listed in the Christian Old Testament) served not only as primary resources for developing specific group practices and beliefs, but they gave sanction and legitimacy to in-house literature written by members of the renewal group as sectarian literature was linked to inherited scripture in both form and content. The Dead Sea Scrolls have provided some 813 part or full texts plus a vast array of fragments from the turn of the common era—biblical texts, deuterocanonical literature, and sectarian materials of hymns and poems, community rules, calendars, liturgies and prayers, apocalyptic works, wisdom literature, biblical interpretations, and books based on the Hebrew Bible. There is an essential link between inherited biblical texts and the sectarian literature found in the Dead Sea Scrolls. The sectarian literature advanced the mandate of inherited scripture in making known the revelation of God for its readership (so much so that the commentary of Habakkuk in the Dead Sea Scrolls claims it can make known all the mysteries of the biblical prophets for its readership [1QpHab 7.1-5]). The rabbis of the first and second centuries C.E. who were heirs to the Pharisaic tradition engaged in a similar literature enterprise, albeit with their own interpretative orientation. All books in the New Testament regularly cite passages from the Old Testament to develop and affirm claims made about Christian practices and beliefs. The point is that the origins of Christianity are set within a religious environment that promoted engaging with inherited scriptures through commentary and exegesis, developing interpretative traditions in both oral and written settings, studying and teaching inherited scripture that were forms of worship and devotion, discovering and refining religious concepts, singing and chanting scriptures, memorizing them—and ultimately writing literature understood to be especially sacred and especially authoritative for the renewal group because it addressed matters of ultimate concern, just like the inherited scriptures. The sectarian literature was a continuum of encounter with the Divine through sacred text and sacred word of study, commentary, interpretation, worship, and writing.

Jesus of Nazareth was as an itinerant teacher in first-century Galilee. He gained a public profile by promoting in both word and deed the imminent coming of a better day (God's kingdom). His small band of followers had turned from other religious possibilities (that is, they "repented"; the Greek term is *metanoé*, "have another mind") to such an extent that they had embraced a view that challenged traditional Judaism. Jesus interpreted inherited scriptures in a radical way; he promised membership in the kingdom of God, not through Temple worship and regular adherence to the Law in scripture, but through belief that he, as an agent of God (as Christ), would be instrumental in bringing about a redefined people of God.[6] This claim was of sufficient substance to make the Romans suspicious that Jesus might disrupt public order; he was arrested and put to death by Roman authorities.

Shortly after his death, his followers encountered Jesus as the resurrected Christ, and this experience was the catalyst for renewed claims of individual and social transformation. The religious renewal activities of Jesus continued in the Jewish homeland with Jerusalem serving as the home base of the movement; leadership was provided by eyewitness followers (disciples) and by those commissioned (apostles) by a Jerusalem council. By the middle of the first century C.E., the Jesus movement extended into the larger Mediterranean world from a home base in Antioch (in ancient Syria), with leadership provided by apostles such as Paul and Barnabas. Schools in the Jesus movement developed around disciples and apostles who advanced their own interpretative emphasis on renewal matters.[7]

It is important to provide these details about the origins of Christianity because the New Testament portion of the Christian

Bible builds on this outline to advance master stories (the Greek term *mythos* means "master story," telling of the decisive events that affect society) affirming that humans can encounter God in thought (for example, through the words of Jesus found in the New Testament gospels), in action (for example, by modeling themselves to be like Jesus and his followers as detailed in the gospels and epistles), and in social institutions (for example, by being member of the *ekklésía*, "church"). Many religions have master stories that are told and retold in family and communal settings, sung in worship, represented in art and architecture, reenacted in rituals—and they are written as especially sacred and especially authoritative. Master stories provide essential foundations for practice and belief by introducing heroes and detailing events about encountering the sacred—and the appropriate response to such circumstances. Claims of ultimate concern are placed within a story, and knowing the story means knowing how to achieve full humanity; the essential feature of master stories is that the hearer, teller, reader, and writer must be able to relate to the story on a personal level in order to deal with questions such as Why am I here?, What is life about?, and What is fundamentally important about life?

Early Christians told and retold stories concerning Jesus in both oral and written forms that included birth narratives, stories about his youth, his public and private sayings, his miracles and the responses of the crowds, his friends and enemies, his arrest and execution, and his resurrection appearances. At some point in the mid-first century prototypes of a distinctive Christian literature called *gospel* (the English word is based on the Anglo-Saxon term *gōd-spell*, "good news") began to circulate in the Jesus movement. By the beginning of the second century four gospels were considered especially sacred and authoritative. Extensive research on the four canonical gospels over the last century suggests that they are interdependent; they agree in *koinè* Greek (common Greek from the turn of the common era) more strongly than when a text is copied from another text. This is true especially of the gospels of Matthew, Mark, and Luke. Yet in their final editions each of the four gospels has its own editorial perspective, unique material, and master stories about Jesus written for a specific audience addressing particular questions of Christian faith and religious practice. Scholars have demonstrated that the final editions of the canonical gospels are end products of earlier stages when sayings and stories about Jesus circulated among his followers in oral and written forms; the written material was crafted less for private reading and more to be read and heard in worship and catechism settings.[8] There seems to have been a literary enterprise in Christian communities to write many gospels (perhaps nineteen or twenty).[9] The four that became especially authoritative and especially sacred reflect stages of Christianity when communities shaped, received, and selected gospels—and, in turn, gospels shaped and created distinctive Christian communities.

When the New Testament canon eventually took its final form by the fourth century, there were twenty-seven books: four gospels presenting the life and times of Jesus; a theological-history called the Acts of the Apostles providing master stories about the life and times of Jesus' first followers and the formation of early Christianity; and twenty-one epistles or letters of correspondence between early Christians on a range of topics giving insight into the dynamics of this emerging religious movement. The New Testament canon also includes a Christian *apocalypse* ("revelation"), the Apocalypse or Revelation of John. The Dead Sea Scrolls confirm that apocalypses were a popular literary genre in Second Temple Judaism; they addressed difficult religious issues, especially in regard to conflict between victims and aggressors, through a particular style of writing. Apocalyptic literature was much like a modern film producer deliberately using black-and-white production to give a certain sense and feel to a story in order to gain a certain response from the audience. The Revelation of John dealt with conflict between the Roman world and Christians, which was understood to be essentially a conflict between good and evil. The Revelation of John warned its readers of hard times coming for Christians who resisted the pagan world, and it did so with all the features of a standard apocalypse (prophetic forecasting of doom, triumph of the righteous and punishment for the wicked, numerology and animal symbolism as keys for understanding the content of the apocalypse).

By the end of the first century all books eventually included in the New Testament canon were in existence. Valued in individual churches and honored in a range of Christian communities because they contained master stories and words of Jesus, as well as teachings of the apostles, they were read in conjunction with Old Testament scriptures, and Old Testament scriptures were read in concert with them, especially on matters dealing with Christology and issues of personal transformation and Christian renewal. They inspired interpretative traditions and were a common source of appeal for determining Christian orthodoxy (right belief) and orthopraxy (right practice). Such determination had become particularly challenging as church membership became not only more Gentile but also culturally and linguistically diversified (important Christian centers were located in North Africa, Egypt, ancient Palestine, Syria, Asia Minor, Greece, and Rome). Various collections of first-century texts circulated among the churches with an emerging apostolic (sanction from apostles) position on how and why they might be used to affirm Christian beliefs and practices as well as to assist in missionary endeavors. Indeed, Christian writings from the second and third centuries regularly used portions of the gospels, epistles, Acts of the Apostles, and Revelation—in some cases indicating they had been memorized (e.g., Clement of Rome, Polycarp of Smyrna, Ignatius of Antioch)—that distinguished them as especially authoritative and especially sacred. They were read interchangeably with Old Testament texts in Christian worship, used as resources for presenting Christianity to pagan state authorities, and functioned as the basis of appeal for in-house doctrinal disputes among Christians. During periods of persecution against Christians in the second, third, and fourth centuries, not only were places of Christian worship destroyed by state authorities, but Christian books from the first century were burned in public, indicating that outsiders were aware of the importance of these texts as authoritative and normative to Christian self-definition. In some cases Christian collections of religious texts were referred to as "the gospel and apostles" in contradistinction to the "Law and Prophets" of the Old Testament, although it is important to emphasize that the twenty-seven books eventually making up the New Testament did not have equal authoritative and sacred status to "the gospel and apostles" portions of these collections (e.g., the Muratorian Fragment discovered in 1740 by the librarian of Milan, Muratori, and dating from the late second century lists some twenty canonical books; Revelation was not popular among churches in Eastern Christianity, and the epistle to the Hebrews had shaky status for Christians in the West). Toward the end of the fourth century a number of factors brought closure to the New Testament canon, including the Emperor Constantine asking Eusebius (Christian historian and apologist; bishop of Caesarea in ancient Palestine) to prepare fifty copies of "the divine scriptures"; Christian councils decreeing that only certain books could be read in churches under the name of "divine scriptures" (e.g., the Council of Carthage in 397); and the translation of the New Testament from Greek into the Latin Vulgate for Western Christianity.

The following list is the traditional arrangement of the New Testament.

The Christian New Testament

Gospels	1. The Gospel according to Matthew
	2. The Gospel according to Mark
	3. The Gospel according to Luke
	4. The Gospel according to John
Theological History, Epistles, or Letters	5. The Acts of the Apostles
	6. The Epistle of Paul to the Romans
	7. The First Letter of Paul to the Corinthians
	8. The Second Letter of Paul to the Corinthians
	9. The Letter of Paul to the Galatians
	10. The Letter of Paul to the Ephesians
	11. The Letter of Paul to the Philippians
	12. The Letter of Paul to the Colossians
	13. The First Letter of Paul to the Thessalonians
	14. The Second Letter of Paul to the Thessalonians
	15. The First Letter of Paul to Timothy
	16. The Second Letter of Paul to Timothy
	17. The Letter of Paul to Titus

	18. The Letter of Paul to Philemon
	19. The Letter to the Hebrews
	20. The Letter of James
	21. The First Letter of Peter
	22. The Second Letter of Peter
	23. The First Letter of John
	24. The Second Letter of John
	25. The Third Letter of John
	26. The Letter of Jude
Apocalypse	27. The Revelation (Apocalypse) of John

The New Testament and the Christian Devotee

Similar to texts in the Christian Old Testament, English and other translations of the New Testament followed earlier Latin editions that were translations of *koinè* Greek manuscripts (some five thousand Greek manuscripts exist of all or part of the New Testament, about three hundred from the second to eighth centuries). Jesus left no literary materials, and he likely spoke Aramaic. Like the veneration of masters and leaders in other religious renewal groups in Second Temple Judaism, early Christians had a sophisticated capacity to remember and pass along important sayings, teachings, and interpretations of Jesus—and the oral and aural features of their missionizing activities were dominant. However, a primacy of sacred language in Christianity—either Aramaic or *koinè* Greek—did not develop, and the devotee could engage with stories and sayings of Jesus and details of heroes of early Christianity through translations in their native language. For many modern English-speaking Protestant Christians the translation of both the Old and New Testaments in the King James Version of 1611 and its revised edition of 1881 is as close as one comes to sacred language through its simplicity, power, and dignity of English prose. Yet it is not without textual defects; it is archaic and sometimes confusing because many of its expressions are obsolete or no longer understood by the common reader. New translations are forthcoming on a regular basis underscoring the principles that (1) Christian scriptures are not a fixed entity, as translations inevitably involve interpretation and commentary of extant manuscripts stated in the vernacular, and (2) they are relational, because translations are driven by the mandate of engagement, providing access to texts deemed especially sacred and especially authoritative in the language of the devotee.

Because early Christians shared the common religio-literary environment of renewal groups in the first century, Christian written scripture emerged to complement the oral and aural features of scripture in missionary, worship, and catechism activities. It has already been noted that Christians regularly drew on Old Testament scriptures to give meaning and substance to claims about Jesus' messiahship; the New Testament was an even richer resource.[10] Christianity eventually understood that Jesus was both God and man. This core concept and central doctrinal tenet was inspired by the New Testament through the blending of master stories in the gospels, which presented Jesus in human circumstances, with essential christological principles in the epistles. As a result, Christian devotees have an immediate and accessible resource for engaging with a foundational concept understood to renew and transform through studying, hearing, and reciting written scripture.

On a counterpoint, it is important to observe that until the modern period (beginning in the sixteenth century) with its print culture based on movable-type letterpress printing (seventeenth/eighteenth centuries), many Christians were illiterate, and even if they could read, access to written scriptures was limited. Devotees heard scripture read to them only in church as part of the eucharistic ritual (taking of bread and wine to commemorate the death and resurrection of Christ) and in other forms of worship. Thus, even though there has been a primacy of written texts for Christianity from the second century onward, the oral and aural dimensions of scripture are—even in the modern era—necessary and fundamental components of Christian scriptures. Since officiating at sacraments and leading worship services are usually done by clergy, the mediation of scripture to devotees by priests and ministers is a central factor for access to sacred word and sacred text. And master stories, symbols, and rituals presented in church worship services and other formal settings profoundly influence how devotees engage with scripture in private reading, interpretation, and application.

The New Testament scriptures are a primary and ongoing resource for affirming a system of multidimensional symbols that inspire deep meaning for the devotee by representing what is essential about Christianity (such as the cross, the infant Jesus, bread and wine, a dove). The symbols represent matters of ultimate concern. Knowledge and understanding of the symbols require skilled insight, wise perception, and sound judgement by the spiritually mature. (Origen of Alexandria, a third-century Christian theologian, outlined three levels of meaning for scripture that apply equally to Christian views on symbols—literal, moral, and spiritual—with the spiritual meaning best discovered by allegorical interpretation.) New Testament symbols encourage devotees critically to think through and reflect on their beliefs and religious practices, especially on how first century symbols from the New Testament apply in a contemporary context. These symbols function as an ongoing continuum linking successive generations of Christians through theology and philosophy. There is a complementary feature of scriptural symbols that is creative and artistic in that they influence the devotee's self-definition and identity by appealing to the experiential and evoking a sense of awe and reverence for what is larger than self. New Testament symbols have inspired devotees to paint and sculpt; to compose and perform music, poetry, drama; and to act out the meaning of symbols, special rituals, and public worship.[11] Some examples are Michelangelo's painting on the ceiling of the Sistine Chapel with its gigantic images of Old Testament prophets foretelling the coming messiah that captures the force of future expectations for Christian self-definition; Leonardo da Vinci's insightful reading of the gospels that resulted in *The Last Supper,* showing Christ as master surrounded by disciples engaged in the mystery and conflict of betrayal; and *The Messiah* by Handel, which inspires a sense of majesty and presence of something larger than self inherent in the Christian view of messianism through musical score, choir, and orchestra presentation.

Most religions promote a holistic view encompassing (1) an understanding of the sacred; (2) depiction of the human condition, usually thought to be somehow flawed or fractured in relationship to the sacred; (3) a way of resolving the human condition through reconciliation and transformation that frequently involves a model person(s) giving direction for resolution; and (4) a path of resolution with theoretical, practical, and social dimensions.[12] Christianity is no exception to this sketch, and New Testament scriptures play a fundamental role in detailing essential factors for the devotee about (1) God and Jesus as Christ; (2) human frailty characterized as sinful and needing resolution; and (3) Jesus' life, death, and resurrection as both model and path for transformation and reconciliation with God. With reference to the path of transformation, New Testament scriptures offer a basis for engaging with theoretical principles with its master stories in the gospels and foundations for Christian doctrines in the epistles and other New Testament texts. They offer models and guides on matters of practice, including baptism, worship, prayer and meditation, and ritual activities associated with Christian sacraments, as well as directives for ethical conduct and moral obligations. The New Testament not only provides an essential basis for reconciliation with God, but it addresses social aspects of transformation regarding how individuals fit into their social and environmental settings and how they understand family, the people of God, and the larger world, as well as how religious transformation and renewal should affect social institutions.

Scripture and the Monastic Traditions

From the fifth to the eighth centuries, Christianity moved from a marginalized new religious movement to the religion of majority in the Mediterranean world; afterward it continued to grow in numbers and influence in Europe. When the Roman Empire collapsed in the fifth century, Christianity emerged as a dominant force in society. It was based in two centers: Rome in the West and Constantinople in the East. Western Christianity eventually called itself Roman Catholic, distinguished by the primacy of the bishop at Rome, and Eastern Christianity took the designation Orthodox, reflecting a confederation of churches located throughout the Byzantine Empire and in the Slavic nations. Whether working in concert with each other or in opposition—they formally separated in 1054—the Bible in

Western and Eastern Christianity increased in importance as the core reference for theological developments and ritual expressions as Christianity moved to center stage internationally, even though it was profoundly diverse in character and membership. The challenge associated with scripture being a core reference for a pluralistic church is well illustrated by linguistic matters. Laypeople in Eastern Christianity who spoke Greek could read some of the *koiné* Greek of the New Testament and the Old Testament based on the Septuagint, if they were literate and fortunate enough to have access to a text. In Slavic majority communities in Eastern Christianity, a translation emerged. However, in Western Christianity laypeople were rather isolated from direct engagement with scripture because Greek was not commonly spoken or read and the Latin of the Vulgate was an ecclesiastical language used primarily by the educated and the clergy.[13]

In both Eastern and Western Christianity, monastic movements followed the model of Christ (based on their reading and interpretation of Matthew 19:21, "If you wish to be perfect, go, sell what you possess, give to the poor and follow me") by selling possessions, providing charity and support to the disadvantaged, and practicing self-discipline in an ascetic lifestyle. In regard to the focus of this study, these movements were not only dedicated to a simple life involving devotion and worship of God through manual labor, regular worship, and meditation, but they sponsored centers of excellence for the preservation of scripture (by copying the Bible) and developed interpretative traditions; they also promoted active engagement with scripture by studying it, memorizing it, reciting it in both meditation and daily labor, and chanting it in prayer and worship. Historically, the monastic tradition was an ongoing source of renewal for Christianity, regularly challenging institutional segments of the religion and challenging itself when it too became an institution. The inspiration for renewal was centered in Christian scripture. As William Graham writes:

> In this monastic discipline [the Pachomian tradition] the life of faith striven for was envisioned as a scriptural life pure and simple. This meant a life permeated and paced, as well as directed and governed, by the living, lively words

> of scripture. The sources indicate that sacred writings were primarily oral in function and aural in impact, rather than written or visual. The total commitment of the life they chose to pursue and their visceral sense of the immediacy of the divine presence were mirrored in the intensity of their preoccupation with scripture and the vividness with which they heard God's voice in its words.[14]

While Graham is addressing the force of oral aspects of scripture in monastic Christianity, it is worth noting that these movements interacted with laypeople in a range of religious and social activities. Thus, they served as models for experiencing sacred word and sacred text for the devotee unable or unwilling to assume a monastic discipline. This also underscores the relational feature of scripture. Even though many lay Christians in the premodern period did not have access to printed copies of the Bible, monastic Christians, through the all-encompassing presence of scripture in their disciplined lifestyle, brokered the biblical message of transformation and renewal through acts of charity to the disadvantaged in a society lacking social services; manual labor in the fields, which provided a commentary on materialism; educational pursuits as forms of worship and devotion; and missionary activities offering hope in an era sometimes referred to as the Dark Ages. The New Testament helped to create and shape the monastic orders, and they in turn shaped and expressed the essence of scripture through devotion and action.

Sermons, Liturgy, Architecture, and Art

The dominant settings for encountering scripture by Christian devotees in the premodern period included the following: (1) liturgy (Latin *liturgia,* Greek *leitourgia,* "public service to the gods"); (2) worship in scripturally based hymns and singing of psalms; (3) repetition of scripture and scripturally derived prayers; (4) catechetical instruction; and (5) the quotation of scripture and its exegesis (Greek *exegesis*, "explanation") in sermons. Scholars regularly observe that the apostle Paul's admonition in Romans 10:17 (that Christian faith is from hearing and hearing is through the preaching of Christ) reflects a self-conscious decision by this religion to promote itself through public proclamation, that is, through public preaching to all who will listen to sermons. This is a feature of Christianity that continues in the modern era. Its primary intent is to make scripture relevant to the hearer in a multifaceted dynamic of Christian theology and dogma, church tradition, prophet-styled calls for renewal, as well as interpretation, exposition, and application of scriptural texts.[15] The point is that there was an interrelation between scripturally inspired liturgy, scripturally derived worship, and scripturally based sermons, on the one hand, and visual presentations of the Bible, on the other. Indeed, architecture and art in this premodern period of Christianity functioned as a primary resource for encounter and engagement with scripture; most visual images were drawn from the Christian Bible. Monasteries and convents were not only centers of intellectual learning, but they supported and promoted a range of artistic forms including metalwork, woodcarving, stonemasonry, drawings and pictures in handwritten Bibles, paintings, and sculptures—where biblical characters and stories were transformed into a visual medium to represent scripture as perceived by the artist.[16] Artists were involved in the design and building of shrines, community centers with biblical themes, churches and cathedrals; they made biblically inspired sculptures and painted scenes drawn from the Bible for their patrons; they made images on walls and windows that broadened the range of how scripture might be perceived. Pictorial and architectural representation of scripture is not about low literacy among premodern Christians; rather, it calls attention to how visual art functions as an effective dimension of scripture in dealing with issues of ultimate concern. Like written, oral, and aural features of scripture, architectural, pictorial, and other expressions of art are relational. The force of biblically based art and architecture would be lost, then and now, if it were not for public reading and knowledge of scripture, recitation, singing biblically based hymns, and educational exposure to the Bible. For the devotee, special attention should be drawn to the preaching and hearing of scripturally based sermons. The dynamic between art and architecture, on the one hand, and the Bible, on the other, suggests that the relational factor of Christian scriptures helped to shape Western culture in its building and artistic expressions. These expressions, in turn, shaped scripture for the masses in a way that rivals the influence of printed Bibles in the modern period.

Scripture, the Protestant Reformation, and Modern Christianity

During the Christian Middle Ages (ca. 500-1500 C.E.) oral and aural features of scripture were fundamental complements to biblical texts in ways even more pronounced than in the ancient Mediterranean world. The combination of (1) widespread illiteracy in society (extending to segments of the clergy); (2) the multi-linguistic nature of medieval Christianity spread across a range of cultures; and (3) the inaccessibility of the Bible because scribal-production was so labor intensive meant that engagement with scripture was essentially an oral activity for most Christians. Of course, orality/aurality were not foreign ideas to a medieval society in which many forms of communication, including texts central to society, were written with the understanding they would be read aloud to the addressee(s) by an intermediate figure representing the sender(s). The reader not only gave voice but also life to the text by reading it aloud.

Many factors in the sixteenth century contributed to changes in Western culture and give reason for referring to that century as the beginning of the modern era. For the sake of this chapter, attention is drawn to the gradual transition from an oral culture in the Middle Ages of Christianity to a book culture in the modern age, when literacy became progressively private and individualistic. That is, there was greater literacy in the early modern period than before among a wide range of people who used writing and books in a variety of personal and public settings including church, government, law, and especially commerce. (A book culture was decisively affirmed with the advent of printing; Johann Gutenberg, a German printer, is credited with printing the first Christian Bible, the Gutenberg Bible, in movable type around 1456 C.E.) There had been earlier indications of this emerging circumstance. For example, in fourteenth-century

England John Wycliffe and his followers, known as Lollards, translated Christian scriptures (and other books) into English to assert that the Bible in the hands of individual Christians was the primary source for Christian beliefs and practices; they were declared heretics as much for their enthusiasm about a book culture as for their theology. John Hus took this theology and the book culture to central Europe in the fifteenth century, and he suffered a fate similar to Wycliffe's.

In the spirit of this emerging book culture, a series of reforms emerged in Western Christianity during the early sixteenth century that gave rise to a protest movement which sought religious renewal by promoting the primacy of scripture (*sola scriptura*, "scripture alone"). The renewal activity eventually resulted in the Protestant Reformation, involving a number of people including Martin Luther (1483-1546), a German monk in Saxony; a Swiss priest, Ulrich Zwingli (1484-1531) in Zurich; and a French reformer in Geneva, John Calvin (1509-64). Along with others, they challenged the interpretive authority of the pope, church councils, and bishops, as well as fellow theologians, by appealing to scripture as the primary and sole reference for Christian beliefs and practices.[17]

For the sake of this study, the point to be noted is that religious renewal,which had been largely conceived and experienced in collective terms during the Middles Ages, focused instead around the individual in the Reformation. Less was viewed as more; simplicity of scriptural interpretation and religious expression were first principles of Protestantism. The Reformation also attempted to recover older or more "primitive" forms of Christianity, especially those thought to reflect Christianity from the first century. (Thus, Protestants reduced the number of books in their version of the Old Testament.) In some segments of the Protestant movement the experiential dimensions of religion became paramount both as a means and a goal of religious renewal. A Pietist movement emerged that linked scripturally based preaching to emotional awakening as confirmation of development and renewal (for example, Methodism formed out of a prayer society in Oxford, England, organized by John and Charles Wesley; it viewed "new birth" conversion as a consequence of plain-styled, scripturally based preaching).

While it is important to acknowledge the impact of the emerging book and individualistic culture on modern Western Christianity—and the religious democratization that resulted from this church-driven book culture—it is wrong to think that the oral and aural features of scripture from the Middle Ages faded into the background after the sixteenth century. Indeed, the Protestant Reformation took the oral/aural features of scripture to new levels for Western Christianity. Printed Bibles in the vernacular language of common people were complements, not replacements, for the oral preaching and aural responses deemed essential for religious renewal. Scripture in translation was intended to be read aloud in public, integrated into public worship, studied in communities of Christians, and used in public forums to address institutional authorities of the church and state. Protestant preachers cultivated a profound aural sensitivity among devotees through skilled scripturally based sermons that took as their point of departure the Romans 10:17 text cited earlier—faith is through hearing, and hearing is through preaching—so much so that Christians who responded to such preaching were viewed as "born again." Vernacular editions of the Bible and prayer books had widespread popularity because they were part of village and town storytelling set in a variety of social gatherings. Memorization of scripture in the vernacular was common among reformers; a new dynamic emerged between the spiritual and the secular realms as scripturally saturated language became part of regular conversation.

The overall consequence of the Protestant Reformation for scripture in the modern Christian period is twofold: (1) It affirmed the centrality of written scripture in both Catholic and Protestant segments of Western Christianity in a manner different from before, that is, in a manner that was modern. Devotees had a printed Bible available in the vernacular, and they engaged with the text in a way that was progressively more private and individualistic (however, it is important to note that private reading was at the earliest a nineteenth-century development, and it may be unique to the twentieth century). This feature of the reforms underscores once again the relational dimension of Christian scriptures. They became less communal and more private and individualistic in the modern period as a consequence of a series of societal developments. The canon of the New Testament, for example, remained the same as it had been for some fourteen centuries, but it was read more as a private scripture than five centuries earlier because modern society held high regard for introspection and self-discovery through personal and private quest. Reduction in the number of books in the Protestant Old Testament is clearly relational, because reformers crafted their Old Testament canon to reflect their attempts to recover the origins of Christianity by matching it to the content of the Hebrew Bible. (2) The interpenetration (that is, mutual flow) between the written and the oral/aural dimensions of scripture was made more effective as a result of the Reformation in Protestantism and the Counter-Reformation in Catholicism. Although contemporary Christians may not be particularly conscious of the oral and aural features of their written scriptures because reading now is generally private and silent, orality/aurality are fundamental to the nature and function of Christian scriptures and have existed in tandem with written scripture since the beginnings of Christianity. The reforms encouraged and made possible engagement with written scripture in a way different from prior time. Only a fraction of devotees over the long history of Christianity actually had read the Bible before the advent of printing, even if they were literate, because it simply was not available to them (the printed vernacular Christian Bible is the most popular book in modern Western society). However, enthusiasm and interest in written scriptures were driven by a factor greater than access, as important as that was. The reforms provided greater interpenetration between written texts and their oral/aural dimensions because people could sing, chant, memorize and recite, discuss and debate, hear and see scripture that was meaningful because it was available in their native languages.

CONCLUSION

The proposition of this chapter is that sacred word and sacred text are experienced by the Christian devotee through central texts deliberately situated in a two-part closed canon. These texts are best referred to as *scripture* because the term underscores the primacy of a written resource as especially sacred and especially authoritative for issues of Christian belief and matters of religious practice. The canon, however, is not a fixed entity—especially in regard to the Old Testament portion of the Christian Bible.

Christians share a common trait with non-Christians in their propensity to scripturalize. Although Christians share a common scriptural inheritance with normative Judaism that is foundational to their self-definition, they deliberately, consciously, and with advanced literary skills wrote texts viewed to be a continuum and fulfillment of Jewish scriptures. These texts contain master stories that advance fundamental principles of religion. They present a clear understanding of an absolute (God and Jesus Christ), views of the human condition in relationship to the absolute, potential for human transformation, and a path for living religiously. Thus, the Christian devotee experiences sacred word and sacred text as a path and guide for life.

Although Christianity advanced the primacy of written texts for its scripture by the end of the first century C.E., until the modern period the vast majority of Christians only heard scriptures read to them or saw them represented in art and architecture that was biblically influenced. This highlights the multidimensional feature of Christian scriptures, especially the oral and aural dimensions that are interdependent with written texts.

Finally, this chapter showed that scripture is relational for Christianity. On a regular basis Christian communities shaped scripture and, in turn, those same communities owe their origins and ongoing development to scripture. This principle is well demonstrated in the modern period of Christianity when the print culture shifted the focus of the Bible from its public and communal emphasis to a progressively more private and individual resource to be used for self-development and personal quest.

Suggested Reading

Coward, Harold. *Sacred Word and Sacred Text: Scripture in World Religions.* Maryknoll, N.Y.: Orbis Books, 1988.

Graham, William A. *Beyond the Written Word: Oral Aspects of Scripture in the History of Religion.* Cambridge: Cambridge University Press, 1987.

Segal, Alan F. *Rebecca's Children: Judaism and Christianity in the Roman World.* Cambridge, Mass.: Harvard University Press, 1986.

Smith, Wilfred Cantwell. "Scripture as Form and Concept: Their Emergence for the Western World." In *Rethinking Scripture: Essays from a Comparative Perspective*, ed. Miriam Levering, 29-57. Albany, N.Y.: State University of New York Press, 1989.

———. "The Study of Religion and the Study of the Bible." In Levering, *Rethinking Scripture*, 18-28.

———. *What Is Scripture? A Comparative Approach.* Minneapolis, Minn.: Fortress Press, 1993.

Van Voorst, Robert E. *Anthology of World Scriptures.* Toronto: Wadsworth Publishing Company, 1997.

Notes

[1] William A. Graham, *Beyond the Written Word* (Cambridge: Cambridge University Press, 1987); Wilfred Cantwell Smith, *What Is Scripture? A Comparative Approach* (Minneapolis, Minn.: Fortress Press, 1993); idem, "Scripture as Form and Concept," in *Rethinking Scripture*, ed. Miriam Levering (Albany, N.Y.: State University of New York Press, 1988), 29-57; idem, "The Study of Religion and the Study of the Bible," in Levering, *Rethinking Scripture*, 18-28; Robert E. Van Voorst, *Anthology of World Scriptures* (Toronto: Wadsworth Publishing Company, 1997).

[2] Smith, *What Is Scripture?*, 16-17.

[3] See E. P. Sanders, *Jesus and Judaism* (Philadelphia: Fortress Press, 1985); idem, *The Historical Figure of Jesus* (New York: Penguin Books, 1993); John P. Meier, *A Marginal Jew: Rethinking the Historical Jesus*, 2 vols. (Toronto: Doubleday, 1991/94).

[4] See Geza Vermes, *The Complete Dead Sea Scrolls in English* (London: Penguin Books, 1997).

[5] Alan F. Segal, *Rebecca's Children* (Cambridge, Mass.: Harvard University Press, 1986).

[6] Sanders, *The Historical Figure of Jesus.*

[7] Raymond E. Brown, *The Community of the Beloved Disciple* (Toronto: Paulist Press, 1979).

[8] See Helmut Koester, *Ancient Christian Gospels: Their History and Development* (Philadelphia: Trinity Press International, 1990); Meier, *A Marginal Jew.*

[9] See John Dominic Crossan, *Four Other Gospels: Shadows on the Contours of Canon* (New York: Winston Press, 1985); Burton L. Mack, *The Lost Gospel: The Book of Q and Christian Origins* (San Francisco: HarperSanFrancisco, 1993).

[10] Reginald H. Fuller, *The Foundations of New Testament Christology* (London: Butterworth, 1965).

[11] Rosemary Woolf, *Art and Doctrine: Essays on Medieval Literature*, ed. Heather O'Donoghue (London: Hambledon Press, 1986).

[12] See Joachim Wach, *The Comparative Study of Religions*, ed. Joseph M. Kitagawa (New York: Columbia University Press, 1958).

[13] Owen Chadwick, ed., *The Pelican History of the Church*, 6 vols. (Harmondsworth: Penguin Books, 1960-70).

[14] Graham, *Beyond the Written Word*, 139.

[15] Harold Coward, *Sacred Word and Sacred Text* (Maryknoll, N.Y.: Orbis Books, 1988),

[16] E. H. Gombrich, *The Story of Art*, 16th ed. (London: Phaidon Press Ltd, 1995).

[17] Robert McAfee Brown, *The Spirit of Protestantism* (New York: Oxford University Press, 1965).

3

The Qur'ān

Hanna Kassis

> *Alif Lam Ra. A Book We have sent down to thee that thou mayest bring forth mankind from the shadows to the light by the leave of their Lord, to the path of the All-mighty, the All-laudable.* (Qur'ān 14:1)

It is reported that the death of the late King Hussein of Jordan was announced to the world by the electronic media a considerable while before an official announcement was made. When questioned about the reasons for the delay, the minister in charge indicated that the official announcement had to be made in the proper manner. By that, it turned out, he meant that the announcement of the death of the king had to be preceded by the recitation of an appropriate passage from the Qur'ān. The momentous event had to yield to the evocation of that which is more pivotal; the contentment of hearing the Divine Word took precedence over the conclusion of a human journey, sad as that may have been. The significance of the Qur'ān as the lifeline of Muslim being, faith, and devotion cannot be overstated.

My purpose in this chapter is not to examine the history of the text of the Qur'ān or its possible sources. Such work, while perhaps valid for its own purposes, has been undertaken by Western scholars with minimal degrees of success since the last century. My task, instead, is to examine the manner in which the Qur'ān is experienced by the devotee.[1] Needless to say, an outsider to Islam, such as I am, cannot fully grasp the depth of ardor felt by one for whom the Qur'ān is the living presence of the divine word. A careful scholar treats the Qur'ān with the deference it justly deserves; a devotee approaches it as the embodiment of the sacred.

The inviolability of religious scriptures is dependent on the believing community acknowledging their sanctity. What, then, were the circumstances that brought a text such as the Qur'ān into the realm of the holy or, as the believer would insist, brought the holy into human hands and hearts? While, according to the believer, sanctity is inherent in the sacred text itself, the integrity of the bearer of the message similarly plays an important role in establishing and maintaining the authenticity and canonicity of the text.

THE REVELATION AND THE MESSENGER: *"SAY... 'THIS KORAN HAS BEEN REVEALED TO ME THAT I MAY WARN YOU THEREBY'" (6:19)*

The Qur'ān is not a book by Muḥammad or about him; unlike that of Moses or Jesus, his biography must be sought outside the sacred book. Rather, according to Muslim belief, the Qur'ān is a book that was revealed to Muḥammad as a means of guidance for the human race. On the strength of Qur'anic support, the hagiographic tradition maintains that the first revelation descended on him on the twenty-seventh night of the month of Ramaḍān (610 C.E.?), subsequently the Muslim month of fasting,

> the month of Ramadan, wherein the Koran was sent down to be a guidance to people, and as clear signs of the Guidance and the Salvation. (2:185)

The significance of the event is such that that night has come to be celebrated as "the Night of Destiny" or "the Night of Power" *(laylat al-qadr)*,

> Behold, We sent it down on the Night of
> Power;
> And what shall teach thee what is the Night
> of Power?
> The Night of Power is better than a thousand
> months;
> In it the angels and the Spirit descend, by the
> leave of their Lord, upon every command.
> Peace it is, till the rising of dawn. (97:1-5)

One traditional narrative of the events surrounding the revelation of the Qur'ān is related by al-Ṭabarī (839-923 C.E.), the Muslim historian and commentator on the Qur'ān. The setting is a cave on Mt. Ḥirā', a few miles north-east of Mecca, to which Muḥammad was accustomed to retire for contemplation,

> The Apostle of God—may God bless him and grant him peace—said, "I heard a voice from heaven saying, 'O Muḥammad! You are God's messenger and I am Gabriel.' I lifted my head towards heaven and behold, there was Gabriel in human form. Then I heard him call from heaven, 'O Muḥammad! You are God's messenger and I am Gabriel.' I stood there looking at him until he disappeared. Then I departed and returned to my family. When I entered my house I came to Khadījah [Muḥammad's wife] and sat down. She asked, 'Where were you?' Then I recounted to her all that I saw and heard."[2]

The chronicler then relates that following recurrences of the episode of call, bewilderment, hesitation, and a return to the shelter of his home,

> Khadījah [Muḥammad's wife] rose, wrapped herself in her clothing, and went hurriedly to her paternal cousin Waraqah ibn Nawfal who was Christian and had studied with scholars of the Torah and the Gospel. She told him what the Messenger of God—may God bless him and grant him peace—reported that he had seen and heard. Waraqah said, "Holy, holy, holy. O Khadījah, he has been visited by

the Great Law (Gabriel) who used to visit Moses. He is the prophet of this people. Tell him to be constant."[3]

Muḥammad returned to Mount Ḥirā' and harkened as Gabriel recited to him the verses that have come to be considered by all Muslims (as well as Western scholarship) as the earliest revelation of the Qur'ān:

> Read/Recite *(iqra')*: In the Name of thy Lord
> who created,
> created Man of a blood-clot.
> Read/Recite: And thy Lord is the Most
> Generous,
> who taught by the Pen,
> taught Man that he knew not. (96:1-5)

This was followed by a hiatus of about two years during which the descent of the revelations ceased. The pause *(fatra)* was sufficiently depressing that, according to his early biographers, Muḥammad, fearing the charge of being demented, contemplated suicide.[4] But eventually he was roused from his discouragement by further revelations returning to him. There is no consensus as to the order in which the immediate next revelations came to Muḥammad. According to the prevailing Muslim tradition, the revelation that followed the hiatus was,

> By the Pen, and what they inscribe,
> thou art not, by the blessing of thy lord,
> a man possessed.
> Surely thou shalt have a wage unfailing;
> surely thou art upon a mighty morality.
> So thou shalt see, and they shall see,
> which of you is the demented. (68:1-6)

Others see either of the following to be the next revelation, the chapter whose incipit is sufficiently hymnic, even in translation,

> O thou shrouded in thy mantle,
> arise, and warn!

Thy Lord magnify
Thy robes purify
And defilement flee. (74:1-4)

or another that sums up vigorously the profundity of the message brought forth by Muḥammad,

By the white forenoon and the brooding
night!
Thy Lord has neither forsaken thee nor hates
thee
and the Last shall be better for thee than the
First.
Thy Lord shall give thee, and thou shalt be
satisfied.
Did He not find thee an orphan, and shelter
thee?
Did He not find thee erring, and guide thee?
Did He not find thee needy, and suffice thee?
As for the orphan, do not oppress him,
and as for the beggar, scold him not;
and as for thy Lord's blessing, declare it.
(93:1-11)

It should be emphasized that Muḥammad had no choice in deciding the occasion, manner, time, location, content, or vocabulary of the revelations that he received. They came to him by varied means. "Sometimes it [a revelation] comes as the ringing of a bell"; Muḥammad reportedly said, "This type is the most painful. When it ceases, I retain what was said."[5]

COMMUNICATING THE MESSAGE: *"O MESSENGER, DELIVER THAT WHICH HAS BEEN SENT DOWN TO THEE FROM THY LORD" (5:67)*

While the chronological order in which the revelations were received should not be overlooked, the divine message *(risālah)* contained in the revelations was, and remains, more significant.

The message was simple and straightforward: God *(Allāh)* alone is God, beside whom there is no other god. One of the earliest revelations, according to prevailing Muslim reckoning,[6] is known as the *Fātiḥah* ("The Opener") and is used as a doxology by the faithful. It sums up the essence of the totality of the revelations,

> In the Name of God, the Merciful, the
> Compassionate
> Praise belongs to God, the Lord of all Being,
> the All-merciful, the All-compassionate,
> the Master of the Day of Doom.
> Thee only we serve; to Thee alone we pray for
> succour.
> Guide us in the straight path,
> the path of those whom Thou hast blessed,
> not of those against whom Thou art wrathful,
> nor of those who are astray. (1:1-7)

Similarly, the new religion is well summed up in the following dictum, albeit contained in a *sūrah* that is considered to have been late in its descent,

> It is not piety, that you turn your faces to the East and to the West. True piety is this: to believe in God, and the Last Day, the angels, the Book, and the Prophets, to give of one's substance, however cherished, to kinsmen, and orphans, the needy, the traveller, beggars, and to ransom the slave, to perform the prayer, to pay the alms. And they who fulfil their covenant when they have engaged in a covenant, and endure with fortitude misfortune, hardship and peril, these are they who are true in their faith, these are the truly godfearing. (2:177)

The impact of the teachings conveyed by Muḥammad may be best assessed by remarks made on behalf of the Muslims by Ja'far ibn Abī Ṭālib, one of the new believers and Muḥammad's cousin, before the Christian king of Abyssinia. According to Muslim tradition, when the well-being of the first Muslims in Mecca was threatened, Muḥammad counseled them to migrate and seek refuge in Christian Abyssinia. Addressing the Negus (king of the Abyssinians) and arguing against the attempt of the Meccan polytheists to have them expelled, Ja'far gave the following appraisal of the impact of Muḥammad and the teachings he brought on the transformation of their lives,

> O King! We were an unenlightened people. We used to worship idols, eat carrion, commit abominable acts, sever the bonds of kinship, treat our neighbours meanly, and the powerful amongst us used to devour the weak. We remained in this state until God sent us a messenger, one of us. We knew his lineage, truthfulness, faithfulness, and purity. He called us to God, to profess belief in His oneness and to serve Him; to repudiate the idols and stones that we and our ancestors used to worship. He adjured us to truthfulness in speech, delivering the trust, maintaining the bonds of kinship, being good neighbours, to abstain from committing unlawful acts or shedding blood; he forbade us the commission of acts of indecency, uttering false testimony, devouring the property of the orphan, or slandering chaste women; he ordained for us prayer, giving alms, and fasting.... Thus we trusted him, accepted him and followed him.[7]

But in spite of this, Muḥammad remained an ordinary man in the minds of his followers, albeit transmuted by the message he was made to bear, "Muhammad is naught but a Messenger; Messengers have passed away before him" (3:144). He was but a prophet and a messenger of God, surpassed by the message he bore. That message was the Qur'ān, the corpus of the revelations that continued to descend on him until 632, the year of his death.

THE LANGUAGE OF THE QUR'ĀN: *"WE HAVE SENT IT DOWN AS AN ARABIC QUR'ĀN" (12:2)*

The Qur'ān, according to its own intrinsic evidence and the consensus of Islam, is God's word revealed to the entire human race in clear Arabic.[8] And although only a small minority of Muslims possess command of Arabic grammar and lexicography, the sacred book continues to be written and recited in that language, which consequently acquired a special position in the Muslim world. Regardless of their differing linguistic backgrounds, Muslims ecstatically hear the Qur'ān recited without necessarily understanding what is said, satisfied by the fact that it is the word of God, seeking its interpretation subsequently.

Whereas several forms of Arabic were current in the Arabian Peninsula during the period of revelation (ca. 610-32 C.E.), the Qur'ān was proclaimed in the Arabic of Quraysh, the tribe to which Muḥammad belonged. At the same time, the Arabic of the Qur'ān stands stylistically apart from any known body of literature in Arabic (or other languages of the Muslim community) and has remained inimitable. The uniqueness of the language of the Qur'ān has become a dominant element in Muslim orthodoxy. Recently, the term *virtual Arabic* has been created and applied to the language of the Qur'ān in order to emphasize that uniqueness and separateness from mainstream Arabic. It is noteworthy that the language and style of the Qur'ān are distinctly different from those of the collected sayings of Muḥammad *(Ḥadīth)*. It is not surprising, therefore, that the notion of inimitability *(i'jāz)* would develop into a fundamental doctrine regarding the Qur'ān. Detractors of Muḥammad were challenged to produce anything similar to it,

> And if you are in doubt concerning that We have sent down on Our servant, then bring a sura like it, and call your witnesses, apart from God, if you are truthful. (2:23)

> Or do they say, "Why, he has forged it"? Say: "Then produce a sura like it, and call on whom you can, apart from God, if you speak truly." (10:38)[9]

STRUCTURE: *"A BOOK WHOSE VERSES ARE SET CLEAR, AND THEN DISTINGUISHED" (11:1)*

The revelations came in one or more small units to which either of two terms may be applied: *āyah* (pl. *āyāt*) or *sūrah* (pl.

suwar). The former term has two different senses. First, it is a "sign" of divine authority in a miraculous form, in the same sense that, according to Christian belief, the healing acts of Jesus Christ, as well as his words, deeds, and very person are also "signs." Second, it is a literary device to identify smaller textual units within the larger literary context of the Qur'ān. Auditively, each *āyah* may be identified by its rhyme or rhythm. Although this is apparent in the written Arabic text, it is more evident in the recitation of the Qur'ān. This element, as well as other aspects of the linguistic beauty of the language of the Qur'ān, is irretrievably lost in translation. It should be noted that, governed by the rhyme, an *āyah* may end while another may begin in the middle of a grammatical sentence. Thus, the end of an *āyah* marks a pause in the recitation of the Qur'ān rather than the termination of an idea, a sentence, or a revelation.

As used in the Qur'ān itself, the term *sūrah* refers primarily to the separate revelations that came down to Muḥammad,

> And when a sura is sent down, saying, "Believe in God, and struggle with His Messenger," the affluent among them ask leave of thee, saying, "Let us be with the tarriers." (9:86)[10]

However, there is another sense that emerges also from the Qur'ān, identifying a *sūrah* as a unit of revelation containing several *āyāt*,

> A sura that We have sent down and appointed; and We have sent down in it signs [*āyāt*], clear signs, that haply you will remember. (24:1)

This sense came to prevail as a literary definition of the term as applied to the physical text of the Qur'ān. Thus, *sūrah* came to mean "chapter," while *āyah* was rendered "verse."

According to Muslim tradition, the position of the various *āyāt* within the *suwar* was ordained by Muḥammad himself. In his meticulous synthesis of Muslim scholarship of the Qur'ān, the noted Egyptian scholar al-Suyūṭī (d. 1505) cites Uthmān, the third Caliph (644-56), under whose authority the extant text of the Qur'ān was collated (see below), as saying, "The Messenger of God—may God bless him and grant him peace—used to say, 'Place these *āyāt* in the *sūrah* in which such and such is mentioned.'"[11] According to another tradition, Muḥammad is reported saying, "Gabriel came to me and commanded me to place this *āyah* [16:90] in this position in the *sūrah*."[12] It is therefore an article of orthodoxy that the constitution of the *suwar* of the Qur'ān was accomplished by Muḥammad, or under his supervision, by the time of his death in 632.

THE CANON OF THE QUR'ĀN: *"NAY, BUT IT IS A GLORIOUS KORAN, IN A GUARDED TABLET" (85:21-22)*

It may be safely said that, depending on their respective sects, Christians use one of three versions of the Bible. The difference among these variants lies in the manner in which a certain number of books—the Apocrypha—are treated.[13] Adherents of Eastern Orthodoxy or Roman Catholicism include some or all of these among the historical, wisdom, and prophetic books of the Bible.[14] Guided by the canon of the Hebrew Bible,[15] these books are excluded from the sacred scripture used by most Christians of the tradition of the Reformation. But the same books are often grouped together under the heading "Apocrypha" in the biblical text used by a third group of Christians that includes some Anglicans, Episcopalians, and others. While all or some of these books are accorded canonical authority in Eastern Orthodoxy and Roman Catholicism, they are read by others "for example of life and instruction of manners; but yet doth it [the church] not apply them to establish any doctrine" (Article VI of the *Thirty Articles of Religion* of Anglicanism). Consequently, an outsider could surmise that Christians are not agreed on the canon of their Bible.

By contrast, the text of the Qur'ān is one and the same for all Muslims, regardless of their sectarian affiliation—Sunni, Shi'ah, or Ahmadī.[16] We have noted that, according to Muslim belief, the canon of the Qur'ān was established under divine guidance by the Prophet, prior to his death, and not by believers at a later time, as is the case with the Hebrew Bible (Old Testament) and the New Testament.[17] Orthodoxy asserts that the Qur'ān in human hands is nothing other than a copy of a "Guarded Tablet" in heaven. But the same orthodoxy also affirms that while the Qur'ān "had been written down in its entirety during the lifetime of the Messenger of God—may God bless him and grant him peace—it was not assembled in one volume nor were the *suwar* arranged."[18]

It is a widely held tradition that since the beginning of the revelation, those of the people of Mecca who were willing to listen to and to accept the message inscribed what they heard in their hearts and recollection, or wrote it down on whatever substance was available to them. Thus, the first stage in the process of preserving and transmitting the text of the Qur'ān rested on two pivots: memorization of the text by the faithful, and its transcription in whole or in part, in legible form, by various individuals.

The exercise of oral tradition in the retention and transmission of a text may be astounding to a contemporary society attuned to the visual means of communication. It is not a surprising achievement in some Near Eastern societies, where it is a common pastime for school children to engage in a poetic contest in which one is required to draw from recollection a line of poetry beginning with the consonant with which his or her competitor's line ended. Such an exercise is not intended to facilitate the retention of a general idea of what is to be passed from one generation to the other within a community, as is the case with the oral tradition of the First Nations of North America. Rather, it seeks the conservation and transmission of an exact text orally. Undoubtedly, human memory can fail and the transmission of one recollector may inadvertently be different from that of another. In addition, varied dialects or forms of pronunciation may present varied readings. In an episode cited by Ṭabarī, Omar, who was to become the second Caliph (634-42 C.E.) after the death of Muḥammad, rebuked a man he heard reciting a certain passage of the Qur'ān in a manner different from the one he himself had learned from Muḥammad. Both men sought arbitration by Muḥammad, who told them that their respective recitations were in accordance with God's revelation.[19] Such variation *(ḥarf)*, sheltered and recognized by the recipient of the revelation, is different from pronunciations that emerged after the death of Muḥammad and in places far removed from Mecca or Medina.

But the conservation of the Qur'ān did not rely entirely on oral tradition. Suyūṭī, mentioned earlier, cites reliable traditions that assert that, in addition to memorization, the text of the revelations was written down during Muḥammad's lifetime and under his supervision. Zayd ibn Thābit, Muḥammad's secretary, is quoted as saying, "We were at the home of the Prophet—may God bless him and grant him peace—collating the Qur'ān from written patches."[20]

There is no doubt that the speech of Quraysh, in which the Qur'ān was revealed, was rendered in a written form in the period preceding Islam. This conclusion may be supported by reference in the Qur'ān to *al-qalam* ("the pen") as an instrument of writing (68:1) and the injunction to write down a debt (2:282), among others. Difficulties in the transmission of the text in written form may arise from the complex nature of writing Arabic. Not unlike other alphabetic languages of the Near East, Arabic was written defectively in a style known as *kūfic*. This is evident from the various extant early Islamic epigraphic remains as well as from the earliest preserved pages of the Qur'ān. By defective we mean that only the consonants were written; the vowels were not. In addition, some consonants, such as *b*, *t*, *th* (as in "thin"), *n*, *y*, or *j*, *h*, *kh*, etc., were not distinguishable from one another; only at a later date were they differentiated by the addition of diacritical marks (points in varying numbers, above or below the shared form of the consonant). Furthermore, diacritical marks such as that to indicate the doubling of a consonant had not been yet introduced. Thus, accuracy in reading a text hinged more on the recognition of the various words as icons than on the decipherment of the components of each word. This is understandable to readers of traditional English where, for example, the icon *gaol* or the varied pronunciations of the component *ough* in different words are recognizable. Dependent on the memorization of the text, the written form becomes nothing more than an *aide de memoir*. Nonetheless, in the absence of faultless recollection, the propensity for error becomes ever present. It is in such a situation that variant readings of a text may develop.

Copies of the Qur'ān were assembled by individuals for their own use. It is not clear whether these included all or part of the text of the sacred book. Among these, it is reported, was a copy compiled by 'Alī, Muḥammad's cousin and *imām* of the Shī'ah, following the death of Muḥammad. According to a contested tradition, he was disquieted by the thought of the text of revelation being tampered with and sequestered himself in his house, except to attend prayer, until he had completed the collation of the Qur'ān. Alternative sources suggest that this meant that he had memorized the text and not that he had committed it to writing.[21]

The collation of the text of the Qur'ān appears to have taken place in three stages. First, there was the text that had been redacted by Zayd ibn Thābit for Muḥammad. It appears that this may not have been a complete collation of the text, as there is mention that Zayd had to assemble the disparate fragments found in the house of Muḥammad and, subsequently, locate people who had memorized passages not written down in his collation.[22]

The second collation was carried out by order of Abū Bakr, the first Caliph (632-34) following the death of Muḥammad. Fearing the loss of the Qur'ān when several of those who had memorized and recited its text died in battle, some Muslims sought its redaction. The leading figure in this regard was Omar, who urged Abū Bakr to arrange for the text to be uniformly written down. Abū Bakr was very reluctant to do what, as he said, the Prophet himself had not done, saying, "By God, had they asked me to move a mountain it would have been a lighter burden than having to assemble the Qur'ān."[23] But in the end he relented and entrusted the task to Zayd ibn Thābit, Muḥammad's secretary, who had himself memorized a sizeable portion of the Qur'ān in his youth, and prepared the first collation. The text thus assembled remained in the possession of Abū Bakr until his death, when it was passed on to Omar. When Omar died, the text was entrusted to his daughter Ḥafṣah.

The third and final collation came about as a result of the clutter of different dialects in the recitation of the text by the various nationalities in the rapidly expanding domain of Islam. For example, difficulties arose between Syrians and Iraqis as each faulted the other group's pronunciation, accusing the other of blasphemy. As a result, Uthmān, the third Caliph (644-56), ordered the collation of the text in the dialect of Quraysh. Borrowing the scroll of the second redaction from Ḥafṣah, he entrusted the task of collation to a team headed by Zayd ibn Thābit, Muḥammad's secretary, whose painstaking attention to accuracy has been held in praise by all Muslims.[24] The resultant text superseded all variants, which were subsequently ordered destroyed. It is generally accepted that the primary achievements of the collation were the elimination of variants that had crept in as a result of mispronunciation, and the ordering of the *suwar*.

THE "VULGATE"[25]—UTHMĀN'S RECENSION: *"A BOOK SENT DOWN TO THEE—SO LET THERE BE NO IMPEDIMENT IN THY BREAST BECAUSE OF IT—TO WARN THEREBY, AND AS A REMINDER TO BELIEVERS" (7:2)*

As it stands since its third and final recension, the Qur'ān contains 114 chapters *(suwar)*, each of which is composed of verses *(āyāt)* ranging in number from 286 (*Sūrah* 2) to as little as ten words in three verses (*Sūrah* 108). With the exception of *Sūrah* 1 *(al-Fātiḥah)*, the *suwar* are arranged according to length, the longest located at the beginning of the Qur'ān and the shortest ones at the end.[26] Readers of the Bible may note a similar practice in the arrangement of the books of the Prophets in the Old Testament, as well as of the epistles in the New Testament.

Each *sūrah* has a title; some have more than one. A title does not necessarily reflect the content of the *sūrah* but may simply be one of the words occurring somewhere in it. The title of each *sūrah* is followed by an annotation indicating the locus of its revelation and the number of verses it contains. In most editions, the chronological position of the *sūrah* is also indicated ("revealed after *sūrah* such and such").

With the exception of *Sūrah* 9, each *sūrah* begins with the invocation, *bismi (A)llāhi r-raḥmāni r-raḥīm*, "In the Name of God, the Merciful, the Compassionate" (known by the acronym *al-basmalah*). In some *suwar* the *basmalah* is followed by one or more letters that are mysterious in their composition and whose exact meaning and function have defied scholarly ability throughout the centuries.[27]

While the *basmalah* and the "mysterious letters" are an integral part of the revealed text, the designation of the locus of revelation is the fruit of Muslim scholarship in the Qur'ān. It is agreed that the components of the Qur'ān were revealed to Muḥammad during two different periods: (1) initially when he was in Mecca (610-622), and (2) after he migrated to Medina and the establishment of the Muslim state (622-32); hence, the designation of the components as "Meccan" *(makkīyah)*, or "Medinan" *(madanīyah)* revelations.

There is a marked difference in tone and content between the earlier and later *suwar*. The earlier revelations are short, vibrant, and rhapsodic. One senses in them the jubilation at the recognition of God's creative and merciful omnipotence, at the mystery, fear, and fascination (to borrow the vocabulary of Rudolf Otto)[28] of the encounter with and submission to God. Clearly articulated are the rewards of paradise for those who believe and the horrors of retribution for those who, having been given the guidance, reject it insolently.

While maintaining the initial themes of the earlier revelations, the Medinan *suwar* contain, in addition, revelations that address the various facets—legal, social, and religious—of the daily life of an organized community living under the rule of God. In addition to religious matters (prayer, fasting, almsgiving, pilgrimage, sin, rewards, punishments, forgiveness, etc.), other issues pertaining to everyday life are also addressed. Ordinances treat such details as marriage, divorce, inheritance, debts, food and drink, slavery, and others. The Medinan *suwar*, whatever their subject, become increasingly developed in style and structure. It would be wrong, however, to thus assume, as is sometimes done, that the rhapsodic language of the earlier period gave way entirely to the elaboration of legal formulations. Needless to say, such differentiation appertains more to the outsider looking at the sacred text. For the insider, the believer for whom it is the word of God, Meccan and Medinan revelations alike are an "inimitable symphony, the very sounds of which move men to tears and ecstasy."[29]

The style of the Qur'ān in both periods of revelation is prosaic but is not prose; it is poetic in that it rhymes but is not poetry. While there are instances of narrative in the Qur'ān, it is not narrative in style. One exception is *Sūrah* 12, which deals with one narrative theme: the story of Joseph. And yet, it is not told as an ordinary story. Similarly, there are frequent references to narrative topics familiar to the reader of the Bible. Without repetition of the details, reference is given to events surrounding some of the major figures of the Old and New Testaments for the purpose of demonstrating God's continued concern for the human race and the latter's persistent rebellion against God.

THE LITURGICAL USE OF THE QUR'ĀN: *"THOSE TO WHOM WE HAVE GIVEN THE BOOK RECITE IT WITH TRUE RECITATION" (2:121)*

We indicated at the beginning of this chapter that a momentous event could not be announced until an appropriate passage from the Qur'ān had been recited. Such is not mere formal ritual; it is an auditive evocation of the Holy that compels a certain degree of protocol and decorum. The first of these is the required purity of the person who handles the Qur'ān,

> It is surely a noble Koran
> in a hidden Book
> none but the purified shall touch,
> a sending down from the Lord of all Being.
> (56:77-80)

As in many similar cases, the exact implication of the term *pure* and what beyond the requisite pure inward intention may be physically required have been left to the interpreters of the Qur'ān to elucidate in different times and places. In some instances it has come to mean physical cleanliness or circumcision (an injunction on all Muslim males).

Following an injunction in the Qur'ān itself,

> When thou recitest the Koran, seek refuge in God from the accursed Satan (16:98)

the "introit" to a recitation begins with the Arabic expression *a'ūdhu bil-(A)llāhi min aš-Šayṭāni r-rajīm* ("I seek refuge in God from the accursed Satan"), followed by the *basmalah*. Upon the completion of the recitation, the proclamation of God's truthfulness is made, *ṣadaqa (A)llāhu l-'aẓīm* ("God has spoken the truth"). The recitation itself, which is usually from recollection and free from error, must be chanted,

> and chant the Koran very distinctly. (73:4)

Reverence is required of cantor and listener alike,

> and when the Koran is recited, give you ear to it and be silent; haply so you will find mercy. (7:204)

It would be altogether wrong to give an impression that the Muslims were only preoccupied with the preservation of the text of the Qur'ān or, now that the text is established, with the ritual of its recitation. It is evident that they engaged equally in exploring its many facets as literature: language, vocabulary, style, occasions of the descent of the individual revelations, and so forth. But the Qur'ān is not simply a literary work, and while all its literary aspects are important, it is the content of the Qur'ān (the Message) that is of foremost significance in the life of Islam and the Muslims. Its precepts shape, guide, and govern the life of Muslim individuals and societies, and reading it or listening to it being recited is an exhortation to abide by its ordinances. It is more than a book, it is the lifeline of a community that has been sustained and nourished by it since its appearance more than fourteen centuries ago. And as much as the implications of the comparison may not be acceptable to Muslim orthodoxy, for the Muslim the Qur'ān is what Jesus Christ, not the Bible, is to the believing Christian. No Muslim would question the Qur'ān's divine revelation, and as a result, it has not been, and cannot be, subjected to the same type of "higher critical" study as has the Bible, whatever the value of that exercise may be to Christianity.

Suggested Reading

‘Azzām, ‘Abd al-Raḥmān. *The Eternal Message of Muḥammad.* Old Greenwich: Devin Adair Publishers, 1964. There is a reissued edition by Caesar Farah and Vincent Sheean. Portland: International Specialized Book Services, 1993.

Cragg, Kenneth. *The Event of the Qur'ān: Islam and Its Scriptures.* Oxford: One World, 1994.

Rahman, Fazlur. *Major Themes of the Qur'ān.* Minneapolis, Minn.: Bibliotheca Islamica, 1994. Also Chicago: Kazi Publications, 1996.

Kassis, Hanna. *A Concordance of the Qur'ān.* Berkeley and Los Angeles: University of California Press, 1983.

Lings, Martin. *Muhammad: His Life Based on the Earliest Sources.* Cambridge: Islamic Texts Society, 1992; reissued Portland: International Specialized Book Services, 1995.

Ṭabāṭabā'ī, ‘Allāmah Sayyid M. H. *The Qur'ān in Islam: Its Impact and Influence on the Life of Muslims.* London: Zahra Publications, 1987; distributed by Routledge and Kegan Paul, London.

Notes

The English interpretation of the Qur'ān used throughout is that of A. J. Arberry, *The Koran Interpreted* (London: Allen and Unwin, 1955). Numerical references in parentheses are to the text of the Qur'ān by "chapter" and "verse."

[1] In addition to summaries of the doctrines of Islam contained in this essay, I quote a text from the *Ḥadīth* (the "Traditions," a compendium of sayings and actions of Muḥammad) that gives a succinct summary of these doctrines, *Muhammad: His Life Based on the Earliest Sources*, trans. Martin Lings (Cambridge: Islamic Texts Society, 1992), 330-31; quoted also by Seyyed Hossein Nasr, *A Young Muslim's Guide to the Modern World* (Chicago: Kazi Publications, 1994), 22.

‘Umar said, "One day when we were sitting with the Messenger of God there came unto us a man whose clothes were of exceeding whiteness and whose hair was of exceeding blackness, nor were there any signs of travel upon him, although none of us knew him. He sat down knee unto knee opposite the Prophet, upon whose thighs he placed the palms of his hands, saying: ‘O Muhammad, tell me what is the surrender *(islām).*' The Messenger of God answered him saying: 'The surrender is to testify that there is no god but God and that Muhammad is God's Messenger, to perform the prayer, bestow the alms, fast in Ramaḍān and make, if thou canst, the pilgrimage to the Holy House.' He said: 'Thou hast spoken truly,' and we were amazed that having questioned him he should corroborate him. Then he said: 'Tell me what is faith *(imān).*' He answered: 'To believe in God and His Angels and His Books and His Messengers and the Last Day, and to believe that no good or evil cometh but by His Providence.' 'Thou hast spoken truly,' he said, and then: 'Tell me what is excellence *(iḥsān).*' He answered: 'To worship God as if thou sawest Him, for if thou seest Him not, yet seeth He thee.' 'Thou hast spoken truly,' he said, and then: 'Tell me of the Hour.' He answered: 'The questioned thereof knoweth no better than the questioner.' He said: 'Then tell me of its signs.' He answered: 'That the slave-girl shall give birth to her mistress; and that those who were but barefoot naked needy herdsmen shall build buildings ever higher and higher.' Then the stranger went away, and I stayed a while after he had gone; and the Prophet said to me: 'O 'Umar, knowest thou the questioner, who he was?' I said: 'God and His Messenger know best.' He said: 'It was Gabriel. He came unto you to teach you your religion.'"

[2] Ṭabarī, *Ta'ṛīkh al-rusul wal-mulūk* ("History of Messengers and Kings"), ed. M. J. De Goeje and others, (Leiden: Brill, 1879-1901), I, 1150 (my translation). An English translation, *The History of al-Ṭabarī* (Albany, N.Y.: State University of New York Press, 1985–) is appearing in separate fascicles. See *Muḥammad at Mecca*, trans and annotated W. Montgomery Watt (1988), 4:71.

[3] Ṭabarī, *Ta'ṛīkh*, I, 1151; *History of al-Ṭabarī*, 6:72.

[4] Ṭabarī, *Ta'ṛīkh*, I, 1155; *History of al-Ṭabarī*, 6:76.

[5] Among others, this is cited by Bukhārī, *Bad' al-Waḥy* ("The Commencement of the Revelation"), Book 2. See *The Encyclopaedia of Islam*, 1st ed. (Leiden: Brill, 1913-1936; reprinted in 1987), 1091-93.

[6] It ranks fifth in Muslim reckoning. Western scholarship makes it a later, the forty-eighth revelation.

[7] 'Abd al-Malik Ibn Hisham (d. 834), *Kitāb sīrat Rasūl Allāh: Das Leben Muhammeds nach Muhammed ibn Ishak*, ed. Heinrich Ferdinand Wüstenfeld (Göttingen, 1858-60), 219 (my translation); English translation, *The Life of Muhammad: A Translation of Ibn Ishaq's Sīrat Rasūl Allāh*, trans. Alfred Guillaume (London: Oxford University Press, 1955), 151. Ibn Hishām edited Ibn Isḥāq's biography (*sīrah*) of Muḥammad (now lost).

[8] Several passages in the Qur'ān are cited in affirmation of this statement. The verse cited as a heading of this section is repeated in 20:113 and, with slight variations, in 13:37 ("an Arabic judgement"),

42:7 ("We have revealed to thee an Arabic Koran"), and 43:3 ("We have made it an Arabic Koran"). The Qur'ān is described as being revealed in an "Arabic tongue" (26:195), "Arabic speech" (16:103), and as "an Arabic Koran, wherein there is no crookedness" (39:28).

[9] Repeated with a slight variation in 11:13, "Or do they say, 'He has forged it'? Say: 'Then bring you ten suras the like of it, forged; and call upon whom you are able, apart from God, if you speak truly.'"

[10] Other illustrations of the use of the term in this sense have already been cited in reference to the challenge to Muḥammad's detractors. See, in addition, 9:64, 124, 127; 24:1; and 47:20.

[11] Jalāl al-Dīn Suyūṭī (d. 1505), *Kitāb al-Itqān fī'ulūm al-Qur'ān* (Cairo: Ḥalabī, 1978), 80.

[12] Suyūṭī, *Itqān*, 80.

[13] The text of the Old Testament used by the early church was that of the Septuagint, the most significant of the Greek translations of the Hebrew scriptures, which was prepared for Ptolemy Philadelphus, the Hellenistic ruler in Egypt (285-46 B.C.E.). It was undoubtedly the text used by St. Paul, and subsequently by Jerome in the preparation of his Vulgate.

[14] The Apocrypha comprises fourteen books, written in Greek or Hebrew during a period extending from 300 B.C.E. to 100 C.E., with the majority being written between 200 B.C.E. and 100 C.E. Jerome recognized their distinction from the canon of the Jewish Bible and gave them the name *apocrypha* ("hidden") without excluding them from the canon of the Old Testament. After 1672 (the Synod of Jerusalem), the Eastern Orthodox Church recognized only four of the books of the Apocrypha as canonical.

[15] The term *canon* refers to those books that are received as scripture being divinely revealed. According to Jewish tradition, the Hebrew canon was closed in the fifth century B.C.E., after the return from the Exile in Babylon (586-39 B.C.E.). More likely, the closure of the canon took place toward the end of the first century, after the destruction of the Temple of Jerusalem in 70 C.E. The Hebrew canon comprises three collections: Torah (the "Five Books of Moses"), Prophets (twenty-one books), and Writings (eleven books).

[16] Sunni and Shī'ah are the two main sects of Islam. Their divergence stems from disagreement, following the death of Muḥammad, regarding the transmission of his authority as leader and guide of the community of faith. The Shī'ah argue that Muḥammad designated his closest kin 'Alī, his cousin and son-in-law, and his descendants as leader (*imām*) of the Muslim community in perpetuity. The Sunnīs, while according 'Alī a place of distinction, argue that leadership was vested in the community itself choosing the best man of Quraysh as leader

(caliph). 'Alī was chosen as the fourth Caliph but was opposed by the nobility of Quraysh, who usurped power and, instead of either proposition for choosing a leader, established a dynastic system of governance.

The Ahmadīs are followers of Mirza Ghulām Ahmad (d. 1908) of Qadiyan (India), who claimed to be the returning Messiah (1891), an *avatār* of Krishna (1904), as well as the reappearance of Muḥammad. After his death, his followers split into two groups over the question of his claim to being a prophet. The latter issue alone was sufficient to prompt their exclusion from Islam, although one of the two groups (Anjuman) asserts that Mirza Ghulam never claimed prophethood. One of the English translations of the Qur'ān, widely used at one time, was prepared by the Ahmadi (Anjuman) Mawlana Muhammad Ali.

[17] The canon of the New Testament primarily implies "standard books of the church." The notion of their being divinely inspired was first introduced by Athanasius (d. 373), one of the "fathers of the church." The canon was established over a period of two and a half centuries, extending from ca. 130 C.E., when the four gospels and thirteen epistles of St. Paul were accepted. It was not until 382, during the papacy of Damasus (d. 384), that a council of the church was held (probably in Rome) which accepted a complete list of the books of the New Testament that were to be considered canonical. Jerome, the secretary of Damasus, was then given the responsibility of revising the text.

[18] Suyūṭī, *Itqān*, I, 76.

[19] Ṭabarī, *Jāmi' al-bayān 'an ta'wīl al-Qur'ān* (Cairo: Muṣṭafá al-Bābī al-Ḥalabī, 1954), I, 13; J. Cooper, *The Commentary on the Qur'ān*, vol. 1, an abridged translation of Ṭabarī's *Jāmi'* (Oxford University Press, 1987), 17.

[20] Suyūṭī, *Itqān*, I, 80.

[21] Suyūṭī, *Itqān*, I, 77.

[22] Suyūṭī, *Itqān*, I, 76.

[23] Suyūṭī, *Itqān*, I, 76.

[24] Details of the procedure adopted by Zayd in copying and verifying the accuracy of the text are recounted in many sources, notably Ṭabarī, *Jāmi' al-bayān*, I, 26f. (Cooper, *Commentary on the Qur'ān*, 25-27), and Suyūṭī, *Itqān*, I, 77-80.

[25] The term, meaning "commonly accepted text," is widely used by Westerners referring to Uthmān's collation, the final recension of the Qur'ān.

[26] Suyūṭī reports that an alternate ordering of the *suwar* had existed, notably that of 'Alī, who had arranged them in accordance with the chronology of their revelation. *Iytqān*, I, 82.

[27] These comprise the following: *a-l-m* (2:1; 3:1; 29:1; 30:1; 31:1; 32:1), *a-l-m-r* (13:1), *a-l-m-ṣ* (7:1), *a-l-r* (10:1; 11:1; 12:1; 14:1; 15:1), *ʿ-s-q* (42:2), *ḥ-m* (40:1; 41:1; 42:1; 43:1; 44:1; 45:1; 46:1), *kāf hā yā ʿayn ṣad* (19:1), *nūn* (68:1), *qāf* (50:1), *ṣād* (38:1), *ṭā hā* (20:1), *ṭā sīn* (27:1), *ṭā sīn mīm* (26:1; 28:1), *yā sīn* (36:1).

[28] Rudolf Otto, *The Idea of the Holy*, trans. John W. Harvey (New York: Oxford University Press, 1958), esp. chaps. 4-5.

[29] Muhammed Marmaduke Pickthall, *Meaning of the Glorious Koran* (New York: A.A. Knopf, 1930 [many subsequent reprints]), translator's foreword.

4

Hinduism

Anantanand Rambachan

In a famous verse from his version of the *Rāmāyaṇa*, the poet Tulasīdāsa writes, "Infinite is God and infinite are his stories, told and heard in diverse ways by the virtuous."[1] In composing this verse the poet was undoubtedly reflecting on the plurality of the Hindu scriptures. "No living tradition," writes Klaus K. Klostermaier, "can claim scriptures as numerous or as ancient as Hinduism."[2] The number and variety of sacred texts in Hinduism are a consistent indicator of the tremendous internal diversity to which the appellation Hinduism refers. This diversity itself is an expression of the antiquity of India and of the wealth of its cultural and linguistic pluralism.

As a world religion, Hinduism is not alone in its diversity, but it certainly has a valid claim to being unique. There is no other tradition sustaining the variety of beliefs, doctrines, rituals, practices, and sacred texts as are contained within Hinduism. While this variety has led some students of Hinduism to question the value of the label itself, the term is here to stay, and it is helpful to think of it as a complex, extended-family name with the suggestiveness and ambiguities of such a name. Family members are identifiable by the possession of shared characteristics, but they are not identical. Like an extended family with a common name, Hinduism is a dynamic movement and flow of the forces of unity and diversity. This fact may be appropriately illustrated by the subject we are discussing. While scriptural diversity is exemplified in the variety of sacred texts within the tradition, unity may be discerned by the arguments through which the authority of these texts is legitimized and in the ways in which they are experienced and used. The Vedas, as we will see, are almost universally acknowledged to be the most sacred and authoritative texts and serve as the norm fot validating the authority of other texts.

MOKṢA: THE HIGHEST GOAL OF HUMAN LIFE

The goal of existence in Hinduism is *mokṣa* (liberation) and various encounters in the sacred literature of Hinduism underline its importance and nature. The *Upaniṣads,* which are dialogues between students and teachers, and which are found at the end of each of the four Vedas, narrate many such encounters. In the *Chāndogya Upaniṣad* (chap. 7) of the *Sāma* Veda, a student, Nārada, goes to his teacher, Sanatkumāra, with a request for instruction. Before teaching him, however, Sanatkumāra asks Nārada to list all the subjects that he has mastered. After providing an exhaustive list, which included grammar, mathematics, logic, ethics and war, Nārada admitted that he was ignorant of the self *(ātman)* and full of sorrow.[3] He asks his teacher for wisdom, which would liberate him from his sorrow. In the *Bṛhadāraṇyaka Upaniṣad* (chap. 2) of the *Yajur* Veda, we encounter the teacher Yājñavalkya and his wives, Maitreyī and Kātyāyanī. Yājñavalkya wants to distribute his property to his wives in order to prepare for his entry into the monastic life, but Maitreyī has a question for her husband. "If I were to possess the entire world filled with wealth," she asks, "would it make me immortal?" Yājñavalkya frankly tells her that she would enjoy a life of luxury, but that she cannot gain immortal life through wealth. "What is the point in getting something that will not make me immortal?" responded Maitreyī. "Tell me, instead, all that you know."[4]

Artha, Kāma and *Dharma* as Secondary Goals

In these typical encounters, Nārada and Maitreyī are not antagonistic to life in the world or reluctant to fulfill traditional obligations as defined by the particular circumstances of their lives. Wealth *(artha)* and pleasure *(kāma)* are two of the four legitimate goals of Hindu life and must be sought within the framework of the third goal, which is *dharma*. While *dharma* is a multidimensional concept, it embraces all that sustains and contributes to harmony in the private and public spheres. The word is derived from the Sanskrit root *dhṛ* ("to support" or "to undergird"), and *dharma* is rooted in the understanding that existence is interdependent and that the efficient functioning of the universe requires human beings to fulfill obligations to God, religious teachers, ancestors, fellow human beings, and nature.

Mokṣa as Liberation from *Avidyā*

There comes a time, however, when one discovers through reflection on one's experiences that the abundance of wealth and pleasure and the fulfillment of social and familial duties do not remove one's sense of want or sorrow. One begins to wonder whether there is more to life than the transient gains of wealth and pleasure and the fulfillment of obligations to the historical human community. This discovery of the limits of the finite and the search for the infinite are really the pursuit of *mokṣa*, the fourth and highest goal of human existence in Hinduism. A Hindu in quest of *mokṣa* traditionally becomes the disciple of a spiritual teacher *(guru)* who is well-versed in the scriptures and who is, as the *Muṇḍaka Upaniṣad* 1.2.12 puts it, established in the infinite *(brahman)*.

A teacher is necessary because of the generally accepted Hindu view that the fundamental human spiritual problem is one of ignorance *(avidyā)*. There is a universal human ignorance about the nature of the self *(ātman)*, the absolute *(brahman)*, and the world *(jagat)*, which is the fundamental cause of human sorrow and want. Freedom from suffering cannot be attained without the right knowledge of reality, and the valid source of this knowledge is the scriptures and, in particular, the Vedas.[5] The Vedas are, in the words of Harold Coward, "the scriptural ladder to release *(mokṣa)*.[6]

Mokṣa as Liberation from *Karma* and *Saṁsāra*

Mokṣa is more than freedom from ignorance and the sorrow that it generates. Ignorance is the primary cause of greed and of actions that are prompted by egocentric desires. Such desires and actions, in addition to their immediate results, also generate appropriate results in the future, either later in this life or in a future one, which the performer must experience. This is the Hindu belief in the doctrine of *karma,* which affirms that every volitional act produces a suitable result for the performer of the action and that the need to experience this result may require rebirth. One is involved, therefore, in a process or cycle of multiple births and deaths, referrred to as *saṁsāra*. The effects of one's actions are never eliminated through experience, since the egocentric actions which are performed in each life continue to produce effects which keep the cycle of *saṁsāra* in motion. Egocentric actions, however, arise from ignorance, and the elimination of ignorance, with the aid of the scripture, brings an end to *karma* and to the cycle of death and rebirth. A liberated person is not generally subject to rebirth.[7]

ORAL AND WRITTEN SCRIPTURE

Śruti and *Smṛti*

For the purpose of understanding the range and character of oral and written scriptures in Hinduism it is useful to employ a traditional orthodox classification of sacred texts into two groups: *śruti* and *smṛti*. *Śruti* literally means "that which is heard," while *smṛti* means "that which is remembered." In this classification the term *śruti* is reserved for those texts that are believed to be revealed and of nonhuman origin, while *smṛti* is used for texts with human authors, regarded as secondary in authority to the *śruti*. While this distinction is helpful for surveying the scriptures of Hinduism, it is important to keep in mind that many *smṛti* texts are understood by particular traditions to be revealed and enjoy considerable authority and prestige within those communities. The Vedas, however, are universally acknowleged by Hindus to be *śruti,* or revealed texts, and continue to be acknowledged as the ultimate religious authority. Acceptance of the authority of the Vedas is commonly regarded as necessary for Hindu orthodoxy, even though such acceptance may be merely formal and nominal.

THE VEDAS AS *ŚRUTI*

The Four Vedas

The word *Veda* comes from the Sanskrit root *vid,* "to know," and literally means "knowledge." In their current form the Vedas exist in four collections, the *Ṛg*, *Sāma, Yajur,* and *Atharva.* This arrangement of scriptural material is traditionally attributed to an ancient sage, Vedavyāsa. Each collection has four sections, the *Saṁhitās, Brāhmaṇas, Āraṇyakas* and *Upaniṣads.* Modern scholars regard this order as a chronological one and consider the *Sahitā* section of the *Ṛg* Veda, dated 1200 B.C.E. or earlier, to be oldest, and the *Upaniṣads*, dated 500 B.C.E. or earlier, to be the latest.[8] The arrangement of the material in four separate collections may be a reflection of the priestly specialization during the performance of Vedic ceremonies centering on fire rituals. The *hotṛ* recited from the *Ṛg* Veda, the *udgātṛ* from the *Sāma* Veda, and the *adhvaryu* supervised the ritual procedure and recited from the *Yajur* Veda. The priests *(atharvan)* who specialized in the *Atharva* Veda performed rituals dealing with the everyday needs of the community to avert difficulties and to ensure success in undertakings.

The *Saṁhitā* portion of each Veda is a collection of hymns addressed to different deities *(devatās).* The *Saṁhitā* of the *Ṛg* Veda, for example, is a collection of 1028 hymns consisting of over 10,000 verses *(ṛcs).* These hymns address and praise *devatās* like *Agni* (*devatā* of fire), *Indra* (*devatā* of the heavens), *Yama* (*devatā* of death) and *Varuṇa* (*devatā* of waters). The *Saṁhitā* section of the *Sāma* Veda contains many of the hymns of the *Ṛg* Veda, but these are set to music with lengthened notes. In recent times Hindu scholars and scholars of Hinduism have been concerned to explain that the plurality of deities in the *Saṁhitā* section of the Vedas does not imply polytheism.[9] The Sanskrit *deva* or *devatā* is commonly translated as God, even though the term *deva* means luminous and refers broadly to a divine entity.[10] *Devatās* are many, but God is one.

The *Brāhmanas* are prose texts that describe the rules for the performance of Vedic rituals. They provide an interpretation of the earlier texts, commenting on the meanings of the hymns, the rituals, and the methods in which particular hymns are to be used, and the results to be achieved.

The *Āraṇyakas* (forest-books) continue the interpretative process already discernible in the *Brāhmanas* by providing symbolic and philosophical reflections on the rituals. Their concern is to direct attention from the outward ritual to their inner meaning and significance.

The trend toward philosophical and spiritual reflection in the *Āraṇyakas* culminates in the *Upaniṣads*, the final section of each of the four Vedas, although the distinction between the *Āraṇyakas* and *Upaniṣads* is not always clear in each collection. The *Bṛhadāraṇyaka Upaniṣad* (Great *Āraṇyaka Upaniṣad*), for example, is both *Āraṇyaka* and *Upaniṣad*.

The word *Upaniṣad* is derived from the Sanskrit root *sad*, which means "to remove" or "to destroy." *Upa* (near) and *ni* (ascertained knowledge) are prefixes. The word therefore suggests a knowledge that destroys human ignorance *(avidyā)* and leads to liberation *(mokṣa)*. The *Upaniṣads* are generally in the form of dialogues between religious teachers and students on the nature of the self *(ātman)*, the absolute *(brahman)*, and the world *(jagat)*. Self-knowledge and not ritual action is presented in *Upaniṣads* as the means to liberation *(mokṣa)* from sorrow and from the cycle of birth, death and rebirth *(saṁsāra)*.

Tradition numbers one hundred and eight *Upaniṣads*, but ten of these have become prominent because of the commentaries on them written by the Advaita (Non-dual) interpreter Śaṅkara (ca. 800 C.E.). These are the *Īśāvāsya, Kena, Kaṭha, Praśna,*

Muṇḍaka, Māṇḍūkya, Taittirīya, Aitareya, Chāndogya, and *Bṛhadāranyaka Upaniṣads.*

The Authority of the Vedas

The Vedas are held to be authoritative within the Hindu tradition because they are designated as revelation or *śruti.* Hindus hold that the universe is without beginning but exists in a cyclical pattern characterized by projection, existence, and dissolution. Like the universe itself, the Vedas are without beginning but are revealed at the start of each cycle of the universe in the same form as they were revealed before. The recipients of the Vedic revelation are the *ṛṣis* (seers), who did not compose the sacred verses but who heard *(śruti)* these eternal Sanskrit words, memorized them, and transmitted them orally to their disciples. A *ṛṣi* (from *dṛś,* "to see") is a *mantra draṣṭa*, a seer of the sacred verses. Through the purification of his or her mental faculties, a *ṛṣi* is able to hear accurately, with the mind's ear, the words of the Vedas in their original intonation and order.

Unlike the *smṛti* texts, which are ascribed to human authors and regarded as having a human origin *(pauruṣeya)*, human authorship is not proposed for the Vedas, and they are spoken of as being *apauruṣeya,* without human origin. The denial of human authorship is another argument for the authority of the texts, since they then become free from human fallibility and limitation. There are important differences, however, in understanding the nonhuman origin of the Vedas. Pūrva Mīmāṁsā, an orthodox school of Vedic exegesis, understands the concept to mean that the Vedas are not the composition of any human being or of God. Pūrva Mīmāṁsā is non-theistic and postulates the universe to be self-existent. Other traditions, however, understand God to be the revealer of the Vedas to the *ṛṣis* at the beginning of each cycle of creation.[11] God reveals the Vedas at the beginning of each cycle of creation in the same linguistic form as they were revealed in the previous creation. The Vedas are not composed or authored by God but revealed by God in their preexistent form.

In addition to their eternal, infallible, and authorless *(apauruṣeya)* character, the words of the Vedas are believed to have an inherent creative power. The Vedic word *(vāc)* is the instrument through which the entire creation is brought forth in each cycle. We may understand this argument better with the help of the exposition of Śañkara.[12] It is a matter of common knowledge, argues Śañkara, that when a person wishes to create a desirable object, he or she first recollects the word signifying it and then produces it. This is also true for the creation of the universe. When the Creator decides to bring forth a new creation after the dissolution of the earlier one, the Creator does so by recollecting the words of the Vedas and bringing forth objects corresponding to these words. God creates the earth, for example, after the Vedic word, *bhūḥ,* occurs in God's mind.

For the Vedānta tradition and Pūrva-Mimāṁsā, Vedic words do not signify particular individual objects, but the *ākṛtis* of these objects. The *ākṛtis* are the essential common characteristics existing in any group of particulars, and these are the primary significance of any word. It is through the common, universal charcteristics that the particular object is recognized. To recognize a particular animal as a horse, for example, one has to first understand the common characteristics of the species; this is what the word *horse* primarily denotes. Particular objects come and go, but the universals are eternal and so are the words that signify them.[13]

The words of the Vedas, which are revealed to or heard by the *ṛṣis* in their eternal order and intonations, retain their creative power and could be utilized for both worldly prosperity and liberation. It is important, therefore, that the words of the Vedas be accurately preserved in their original sequence and intonation. This was and continues to be the sacred task entrusted to *brahmin* priests. Proper intonation can only be preserved by hearing the texts, and the Vedas were memorized and transmitted in oral form from teacher to student. The *Ṛg* Veda was first printed in a book in the nineteenth century through the efforts of European Indologist F. Max Müller, and he primarily relied on the memories of *brahmin* specialists and not on manuscripts.

While it is true that traditions which are transmitted orally reflect the improvisations of the individual reciters, this did not hold true for the Vedas. The Hindu understanding of the eternity and power of the text led to the development of sophisticated techniques for ensuring unaltered transmission and the correct performance of rituals. Six ancillary disciplines emerged, referred to collectively as the *Vedāṅgas* or limbs of the Vedas. While these are not a part of the Vedas, they are considered indispensable for the proper recitation, understanding, and use of the Vedas.

The Six *Vedāṅgas*

Śikṣa (phonetics) deals with the rules of faultless pronunciation and accentuation of the Vedic *mantras*. Two of the more comprehensive *śikṣa* texts are the *Pāṇinīya Śikṣa* and the *Yājñavalkya Śikṣa*.

Mantras that are incorrectly intonated will not produce desirable meanings or effects. There is a well-known story about a ritualist named Tvaṣṭā, who wanted an *asura* (demon) to destroy Indra. Because of incorrect recitation, the opposite effect was produced and the *asura* was killed by Indra. Vedic words are chanted in three tones, low *(anudātta)*, high *(udātta)*, and middle *(svarita)*. Accuracy is preserved by employing a variety of chanting techniques. *Saṁhitāpāṭha* is the continuous chanting of *mantras* without breaking word-combinations *(sandhis)*. In the method of *padapāṭha*, the *mantras* are chanted by breaking the word-combinations and reciting each individual word. *Kramapṭāha* is a method of chanting by joining two words until the entire verse is recited. The use of different recitation methods served as a way of checking the accuracy of individual words and their relationship to preceding and subsequent ones.

Vyākaraṇam is the study of grammar and a seminal text in this regard is the *Aṣṭādhyāyī* of Pāṇini (ca. fifth to sixth centuries B.C.E.). Since the Vedas are in the form of words, the study of Sanskrit grammar is considered indispensable for the understanding of the texts and many traditional temples have a special hall *(vyākaraṇa dāna maṇḍapam)* for the study of grammar.

Chandas deals with the various meters in Sanskrit. The earliest work on *chandas* was written by Pingalanāga (ca. fifth to sixth centuries B.C.E.). There are seven meters in the Vedas, and the use of these facilitated memorization of the texts as well as their preservation.

Niruktam (etymology) is concerned with explaining the meaning of difficult Vedic words. The earliest available work is the *Nirukta* of Yāksa (before sixth century B.C.E.), which deals with the etymology of Vedic words contained in an earlier collection, the *Nighaṇṭu*. Yāksa also includes explanations of words from other Vedic verses.

Jyotiṣam (astronomy and astrology) helps to set the proper times for the performance of Vedic rituals. To be successful, these rituals must be performed at designated planetary configurations. Lagadha's *Jyotiṣavedāṇga* (ca.400 B.C.E.) is one of the earliest works dealing with this topic. Other works were authored by Āryabhaṭṭa (fifth century C.E.) and Bhāskarācārya (twelfth century C.E.).

Kalpam discusses the details of Vedic rituals. This limb of the Vedas is concerned with the proper procedures for each ritual, when and which *mantras* are to be recited, the material to be offered, and the types of priests required. The ritual manuals are collectively referred to as the *Kalpasūtras* and include the *Śrautasūtras* (dealing with public ritual), the *Gṛhasūtras* (dealing with domestic ritual), and the *Dharmasūtras* (dealing with religious law).

SMṚTI: THE REMEMBERED SCRIPTURES

While the Vedas continue to enjoy supreme canonical status within Hinduism, it is true that the majority of Hindus encounter the material of the Vedas indirectly through the *smṛti* texts. Traditional study of the Vedas was limited to the male members of the first three castes *(brahmaṇas, kṣatriyas,* and *vaiśyas). Śūdras* and women were traditionally excluded from the study and hearing of the Vedas and were exposed only to the *smṛti* literature. *Smṛti* texts generally legitimized their status by linking themselves to the authority of the Vedas, and all of them seek, in one way or another, to claim the sanction of the Vedas for their particular teachings. The vast number of texts that are classified as *smṛti* precludes detailed discussion or even enumeration. We will focus on those that continue to be significant at the popular level.

Itihāsa

The Sanskrit term *itihāsa* means "thus indeed it was" (*iti* [thus] *ha* [indeed] *āsa* [it was]). It is a collective term used for the *Rāmāyaṇa* and the *Mahābhārata*, commonly referred to as the Epics.

The *Mahābhārata* (400 B.C.E.–400 C.E.) is traditionally attributed to Vyāsa, although the name itself simply means "compiler." It is considered to be the longest work in Indian literary history and consists of over 100,000 verses. It is four times as large as the Bible and eight times the length of the Greek epics, the *Iliad* and the *Odyssey*, combined. The text claims to be comprehensive in its content: "Whatever is written here may also be found elsewhere; but what is not found here cannot be found anywhere else either *(yad ihāsti tad anyatra yad nehāsti na tat kva cit)*." It is popularly regarded as the fifth Veda *(pañcamo Veda)*, thus linking its authority to that of the Vedas.

The main story of the *Mahābhārata* is clear, even though the text also relates myths and events not connected with the central narrative. This narrative recounts the struggle between two sets of cousins, the Pāṇḍavas and the Kauravas, for a kingdom in North India. The Kaurava leader, Duryodhana, is power-hungry and reluctant to do justice to his cousins. After futile efforts for a peaceful resolution, the parties engage in a climactic battle at Kurukṣetra in which most of the warriors on both sides are slaughtered, but from which the Pāṇḍavas emerge victorious.

One of the enduring legacies of the *Mahābhārata* is the *Bhavagadgītā* ("Song of God"). The *Bhagavadgītā* (150 B.C.E.–250 C.E.), now widely abbreviated as the *Gītā*, is a dialogue of 700 verses, arranged in eighteen chapters, between Kṛṣṇa and his Pāṇḍava friend, Arjuna. It constitutes chapters 23-40 of the *Bhīṣmaparvan* (Book 6) of the *Mahābhārata*. On the day of the great battle, Kṛṣṇa, who has volunteered to serve as Arjuna's charioteer, is instructed by Arjuna to drive his chariot between the two armies so that he can survey the opposing forces. The prospect of having to fight against his relatives and teachers saps all enthusiasm from Arjuna and throws him into a moral crisis. Kṛṣṇa uses this moment to instruct Arjuna about the immortality of the self and the necessity of fulfilling his social duty *(svadharma)* as a warrior. Perfoming actions without selfish and egocentric motives is conducive to the attainment of liberation.

The authority of the *Bhagavadgītā* is undoubtedly connected with the fact that Arjuna eventually discovers (chapter 11) that his advisor is none other than God, in one of his human incarnations *(avatāra)*. Even though formally a *smṛti,* the text is revered as the word of God and treated by its earliest commentators as revelation. Each chapter of the text concludes with a colophon extolling the text as an *upaniṣad* and connecting it to the last sections of the Vedas. Kṛṣṇa himself presents his teachings to Arjuna as a restatement of earlier revelations.

Rāmāyaṇa

The *Rāmāyaṇa* (400 B.C.E.–300 C.E.) is about a quarter of the length of the *Mahābhārata*; it is traditionally attributed to the poet Vālmīki. It consists of seven books *(kāṇḍas)* narrating the life story of Rāma, incarnation of Viṣṇu and prince of the north Indian kingdom of Ayodhyā. Rāma, heir to the throne of Ayodhyā, is banished into exile at the request of his stepmother, Kaikeyī, who wishes for her own son, Bharata, to be the king. Rāma calmly accepts his banishment because a promise of his father, Daśaratha, to his stepmother was at stake. He is acompanied by his wife, Sītā, and his brother, Lakṣmaṇa. During their wandering as ascetics, Sītā is kidnapped by Rāvaṇa, the king of Śrī Lañka, and taken to his island home. Rāma assembles an army, rescues Sītā and returns to rule Ayodhyā.

The *Rāmāyaṇa* has been described as the Hindu's favorite book and Rāma and Sītā are venerated as models of virtue *(dharma)*, exemplifying filial obedience, brotherly love, and loyalty in marriage. There are vernacular versions in all the major languages of India, but the most popular is the *Rāmacaritamānas* of Tulasīdāsa (sixteenth century). Tulasīdāsa composed his version of the text in an eastern Hindi dialect known as Avadhī. He used the style of *caupāīs* (verses with four lines) and *dohās* (couplets) to tell his story of Rāma. The use of the vernacular and rhyme contributed to the ascendancy of Tulasīdāsa's version. He claims his text to be in accord with the Vedas, although he uses the term to include the four Vedas as well as other *smṛti* texts.

Purāṇas

Purāṇa (old, ancient) is the general term used for a group of eighteen Sanskrit texts compiled between 400 C.E. and 1000 C.E. Like the *Mahābhārata* and the *Rāmāyana*, the *Purāṇas* could be heard by all, and they have deeply influenced the popular understanding and practice of Hinduism. As a genre of religious literature the *Purāṇas* are supposed to deal with five subjects *(pañca lakṣaṇas)*: the origin of creation; the dissolution of the universe and its re-creation; genealogies of sages, kings, and deities; cosmic cycles ruled by the Manus; and the history of solar and lunar dynasties.[14]

The eighteen *Purāṇas* contain a total of 400,000 verses; each is generally centered on one or another of the major deities of Hinduism—Viṣṇu, Śiva, or Śakti (the Goddess). Devotees of a particular deity tend to selectively give emphasis and importance to the *Purāṇa* extolling that deity. Devotees of God as Viṣṇu, especially in Viṣṇu's incarnation as Kṛṣṇa give priority to the *Bhāgavata Purāṇa*, especially the tenth chapter, which narrates the life of Kṛṣṇa. The followers of the International Society for Kṛṣṇa Consciousness (ISKCON), a Vaiṣṇava devotional movement founded in New York in 1966, include this *Purāṇa* in the category of what they regard as the Vedic scriptures.

Āgamas AND *Tantras*

While the term *āgama* is used broadly for a sacred text, it is employed more specifically to indicate a large body of scriptural literature dating from the seventh to the eleventh centuies C.E. Like the *Purāṇas*, the *Āgamas* center on the principal Hindu deities—Viṣṇu, Śiva, and Śakti—and are considered by their respective communities to be revealed.

The Vaiṣṇava *Āgamas*, centered on the worship of God as Viṣṇu, are known as the *Pāñcarātras* (or *Saṁhitās*), and the tradition lists one hundred and eight texts. They provide details relating to construction of Hindu temples and the conduct of festivals and worship rituals. Many famous temples in India such as the Bālāji temple in Tirupati and the Rañganātha Temple in Śrīraṇgam, follow the *Pāñcarātras* in their worship practices.

The Śaiva *Āgamas* deal with the worship of God as Śiva and take the form of a dialogue between Śiva and his *śakti*, the goddess Pārvati. There are twenty-eight Śaiva *Āgamas*, and the two major traditions of Śaivism (Śaiva Siddhanta in Southern India and Kāśmīr Śaivism in Northen India) regard the *Āgamas* as authoritative. The Śaiva *Āgamas* are divided into four parts, *vidyāpāda* (the knowledge of Śiva), *kriyāpāda* (temple construction and worship rituals), *yogapāda* (disciplines for attaining union with Śiva), and *cāryāpāda* (daily conduct).

The Śakta *Āgamas* are called *Tantras* and focus on the worship of the Goddess *(Śakti)*. The seventy-seven Śakta *Āgamas* represent the Goddess as supreme and hold union with her to be the goal of human existence. The *Tantras* present an elaborate and graded path to liberation consisting of ritual worship, chanting, *mantra* recitation, and meditation. These practices, however, must be undertaken under the guidance of a teacher and only after proper initiation *(dīkṣa)*.

Sacred Literature in the Vernacular

In all of the regional languages of India there are devotional works that are extremely popular. Their availability in the local dialects, as opposed to Sanskrit, enhanced their appeal.

In South India the *Divyaprabandham*, which is a collection of the songs of the Vaiṣṇava devotional poets known as the Ālvārs (500-850 C.E.), the *Tevāram*, which contains the songs of Sambandhar, Appar, and Sundarar (600-750 C.E.), and the *Tiruvācakam*, containing the compositions of Māṇikka Vācakar (seventh century C.E.) are among the most important devotional works in Tamil. Songs from these collections are widely used in daily temple and home worship. In Kannada, there is a large collection of devotional songs composed between the fifteenth and eighteenth centuries by poets such as Purandaradāsa, Kanakadāsa, Vijayadāsa, Gopāladāsa, and Jagannāthadāsa. The Telugu compositions of Tyāgarāja are treasured for their spiritual insight and musical creativity. Popular in Kerala are the songs of Irayimman Thambi, court poet of Svāti Tirunāl (1829-47 C.E.).

In North India poetic compositions in Hindi and its various dialects live in the memories and daily recitations of millions. Among the well-known devotional poets of North India are Sūrdās (sixteenth century C.E.), Kabirdās (fifteenth century C.E.), Mīrabāi (sixteenth century C.E.), and Tulasīdāsa (sixteenth century C.E.).[15] The *abhañgas* of Tukārām (seventeenth century C.E.) in Marathi and Gujerati songs of Narsi Mehta (sixteenth century C.E.) are recited daily. A relatively recent composition, like the *Gītāñjali* of Rabindranath Tagore (1861-1941), India's Nobel laureate, has already taken its place among India's devotional works. In its orginal Bengali and English translations it is used in liturgical settings.

The Experience of Scripture in the Life of the Devotee

The scriptures of Hinduism, as already indicated, are experienced by the devotee primarily through hearing the sacred words. Various reasons have been suggested for the low status of written texts in India.[16] Coward points to the introduction of writing from outside, the removal of the necessity for a guru, the significance of sound, and the difficulty of preserving palm leaf and birch bark manuscripts in the tropics as some reasons for the early Hindu antipathy toward the written. To all of these we must add also the factor of caste which worked to limit literacy to the higher groups. The scriptures could only be heard by the masses, because they could not read.

Memorization and Repetition of Scripture

Memorization and repetition of the Vedas continue to be an important feature in the life of Hindus of the upper castes. Young boys from these families commonly undergo the sacrament *(saṁskāra)* of *upanayana,* at which they are invested with the sacred thread *(yajñopavīta)* and commence memorization of the Vedas. This is the occasion also for receiving the *Gāyatrī mantra,* which is then recited daily.[17] Study, recitation, and teaching of the Vedas are religious obligations which confer well-being here and in the hereafter. These are the means also for discharging one's debt to the *ṛṣis*.

Although study and recitation of the Vedas have been the preserve of upper-caste Hindus, reform movements have made a difference in this regard. One of these is the Arya Samaj, which was founded by Swami Dayananda Sarasvati (1824-83). Dayananda Sarasvati rejected the authority of the *smṛtis* and championed the *saṁhitā* section of the Vedas as being the original and true revelation. While there are certain ambiguites in Dayananda's views on caste, he argued that caste should be determined by an individual's nature, qualities, and actions. The study of the Vedas was open to all interested persons. The Arya Samaj founded schools in many parts of India and also among Hindu communities outside of India, where the attempt is made to combine traditional Vedic education with Western learning. The *agnihotra* (Vedic fire ritual) is the basic mode of worship for members of this group. Offerings are made to God through the sacred fire, with the recitation of *mantras* from the Vedas. The Arya Samaj continues to make a significant contribution to the use of the Vedas in Hindu worship.

The tradition of memorizing and reciting the Vedas has influenced similar practices with other texts. Parts of texts such as the *Bhagavadgītā* and the *Rāmacaritamānasa* of Tulasīdāsa are memorized and recited as part of domestic and public worship. The fifteenth chapter of the *Bhagavadgītā* is recited before meals in many Hindu monasteries *(āśramas)* while the *Sundarakāṇḍa* (fifth chapter) of the *Rāmacaritamānasa* is regularly recited in Hindu homes for domestic happiness. In North India millions of Hindus have memorized and recite daily the *Hanumāncālīsā*, a short poem attributed to Tulasīdāsa, in praise of Hanumān, a servant and devotee of Rāma.

The Use of Scripture in Ritual

In addition to memorization and recitation, Hindus also experience their scripture in public and private ritual. Life-cycle rites (birth, initiation, marriage, death) still follow the traditions of the Vedas. Public and private worship in homes and temples involving the consecration and use of icons *(mūrti)* follow procedures specified in the *Āgamas,* with *mantras* drawn from both the Vedas and *Āgamas*. The most popular form of Hindu worship, the *pūúā*, which is a ritual of sixteen hospitality offerings made in the presence of an icon, is derived from *Āgamic* sources.

The general term used for a Vedic worship ritual is *yajña*, which is derived from the root *yaj* (to worship). The various *yajñas* prescribed in the Vedas may be broadly classifed into those that are obligatory and those that are nonobligatory. Obligatory *yajñas* include those that must be done on a daily basis *(nitya karmas)* and those that have to be done occasionally *(naimittika karmas)*. One example of a *nitya karma* is *sandhyāvandanam*, which is to be performed at dawn, noon, and dusk, and during which the *Gāyatrī mantra* is recited. One example of an occasional obligatory ritual is the annual *śrāddha* ceremony done in memory of departed ancestors. Nonobligatory rituals *(kāmya karma)* include those like the *putrakāmeṣṭi yajña* for the birth of a son, and the *aśvamedha yajña* traditionally performed by a ruler for the attainment of sovereignty.

Yajñas are performed with the faith that the *mantras* of the Vedas, when properly chanted in a ritual context, produce their expected result. The words of the Vedas, as we have already noted, are believed to be eternal creative sounds and are the words out of which the creation itself emerged. The efficacy of sacred verses in a ritual context does not depend upon the reciter understanding the word meanings. In traditional methods of reciting and memorizing the Vedas, precise intonation matters above all else.

The Use of Scripture for Japa

In addition to the memorization and repetition of scripture and its use in a ritual context, it is a common Hindu practice to chant repeatedly a single word or a brief verse from the scripture. This practice is referred to as *japa* and may be done audibly *(ucca japa)*, orally but inaudibly *(manda japa)*, and mentally *(citta japa)*. Since one is repeating a brief verse, *japa* is not a feat of memory. The repetition of the *mantra* is usually done with the aid of a *japa mālā* or rosary, generally made up of 108 beads. A single bead is moved forward with each chant, until the *mālā* is completed. The process may then be repeated.

The *mantras* used by Hindus for *japa* are usually received from the *guru* at the time of initiation. Upper-caste Hindu boys receive the *Gāyatrī mantra* from the teacher at the time of the *upanayana* ceremony. Through this ceremony the initiate becomes eligible to study the Vedas and is required to recite the *Gāyātri mantra* daily. Any Hindu, however, may choose to receive *mantra-dikṣā* or initiation with a *mantra* from a *guru* of his or her choice.[18] The *mantra* is selected by the *guru* for its appropriateness to the spiritual needs of the disciple and softly whispered into the right ear at the time of the initiation ceremony. A *mantra* received in this manner from a *guru* is believed to be potent. It must be kept a secret and used appropriately. It is not uncommon, however, for Hindus to select a favorite scriptural verse or the name of a chosen deity for the purposes of *japa*.

Scriptural verses and words are used in *japa* for a variety of purposes. *Japa* is a daily part of the obligatory worship for many and is seen as a great aid to freeing the mind from distractions and centering it on God. The devotional *(bhakti)* traditions of Hinduism give great emphasis to the religious value of repeating the name of God. *Japa* may also be done as part of a vow *(vrata)*, either before or after a particular end has been achieved. It is frequently done at times of serious illness or impending death with the hope of effecting recovery or creating the awareness of God in the mind of the dying. Hindus believe that if one's mind is fixed on God at the time of death, one attains God.[19]

The Use of Scripture as a Valid Source of Knowledge *(Pramāṇa)*

I have described the use and experience of scripture in various contexts in which primary emphasis is upon correct pronunciation rather than meaning. This may give the wrong impression that ascertaining the meaning of scripture is irrelevant or unimportant. This is far from the truth, as a well-known verse from the *Manusmṛti* (12:103) emphasizes:

> (Even forgetful) students of the (sacred) books are more distinguished than the ignorant, those who remember them surpass the (forgetful) students, those who possess

a knowledge (of the meaning) are more distinguished than those who (only) remember (the words), men who follow (the teaching of the texts) surpass those who (merely) know (their meaning).[20]

In the well-known dialogue between Yājñavalkya and Maitreyī (2.4.5) in the *Bṛhadāraṇyaka Upaniṣad*, Yājñavalkya states that the teaching of the text must be heard *(śravaṇa)*, reflected upon *(manana)*, and contemplated *(nididhyāsana)*. At the end of the *Bhagavadgītā* (18:72) Kṛṣṇa asked Arjuna if he had listened to his teaching with an attentive mind and if his ignorance and confusion had been dispelled. He also praises the study of the text and teaching it to qualified seekers.

The six classical orthodox traditions of India regard the Vedas as a source of valid knowledge *(pramāṇa)*. While they are not in agreement on the number and nature of the valid sources of knowledge, all six include scripture *(śabda pramāṇa)*.[21] Among the six schools, however, it the Pūrva Mīmāṁsā and the Vedānta traditions that are primarily schools of Vedic exegesis and for whom right understanding of the meaning of the texts is crucial to the attainment of liberation *(mokṣa)*.

Pūrva Mīmāṁsā AND *Uttara Mīmāṁsā*

As far as the tradition of Pūrva Mīmāṁsā is concerned, the Vedas are only a *pramāṇa* for the revelation of *dharma* or religious duty. Religious duty in the Vedas is expressed in the form of positive commands *(vidhi)* and negative commands *(niṣedha)*.[22] It is from the Vedas alone that we learn about the connection between particular actions and the unseen results they produce. The intention of the Vedas is to instigate right ritual and social action and the avoidance of improper ones. All words in the Vedas, according to Mīmāṁsā exegetes, have meaning only in relation to action; they are meaningless if some connection cannot be demonstrated with the injunctive texts. The words of the Vedas are not concerned with just providing information about existing realities.

With these assumptions about the nature of the Veda as a source of knowledge, Pūrva Mīmāṁsā give primary importance to the first three sections of the Vedas (*Saṁhitās*, *Brahmaṇas* and *Āraṇyakas*) and secondary value to the *Upaniṣads*. The *Upaniṣads* are regarded as merely an appendage to the first three sections of the Vedas and provide information that is supplementary to these texts. They are not understood to have any independent subject matter.

This interpretation of the nature and purpose of the Vedas was challenged by the Vedānta or Uttara Mīmāṁsā schools and most strongly by the Advaita (non-dual) tradition, whose principal exponent was Śaṅkara (ca.800 C.E.). While agreeing with the ritualists that the Vedas are a *pramāṇa* for *dharma*, he argues, however, that this is the legitimate subject matter of the first three sections of the Vedas, which he collectively refers to as the *karmakāṇḍa* (ritual section). The *Upaniṣads*, on the other hand, which comprise the *jñānakāṇḍa* (knowledge section), have an entirely different subject matter, which is the revelation of the absolute (*brahman*). Although *brahman* is an existent reality, it does not possess any qualities that could be apprehended through the senses and cannot be known in the manner of ordinary objects. Without data from the senses, we cannot make any reliable inferences about the nature of *brahman*. The words of the Vedas, and, in particular, the *Upaniṣads*, constitute a valid means for knowing *brahman*.[23]

For Śaṅkara, *brahman* is free from limitations of all kinds and identical with the human self (*ātman*). Because of ignorance, the human self is identified with the limited body and mind and the individual becomes subject to sorrow (*duḥkha*) and *saṁsāra*, the cycles of birth, death, and rebirth. Liberation (*mokṣa*) is attained as a consequence of understanding the identity of the *ātman* and *brahman*. The revelation of this identity, for Śaṅkara, is the central purport of the *Upaniṣads*. Along with the *Upaniṣads*, the Advaita tradition looks to *Brahmasūtras* of Bādarāyaṇa (second century C.E.) and to *Bhagavadgītā* as authoritative sources for its viewpoint. These three sources are collectively referred to as the *prasthāna trayi*, or the triple foundation of the Vedānta.

Many aspects of Śaṅkara's interpretation of the *Upaniṣads* were questioned by later commentators. One of Śaṅkara's most vigorous critics was Rāmānuja (1017-1137 C.E.), exponent of the Viśiṣṭādvaita (qualified non-dual) tradition of Vedānta. Unlike Śaṅkara, who subordinated the first three sections of the Vedas to the final section, the *Upaniṣads*, Rāmānuja treated all sections as having equal value. He sought to refute Śaṅkara's understanding of the identity of *brahman* and *ātman* by claiming that the texts expound a doctrine of inseparability *(apṛthak siddhi)* and not identity. While agreeing with Śaṅkara that *brahman* is non-dual *(advaita)*, Rāmānuja argued that *brahman* was internally diverse and complex. The all-inclusive *brahman* contains within itself matter *(acit)* and individual selves *(cit)*. These are really distinct from each other but completely dependent upon and inseparable from *brahman*.

Liberation *(mokṣa)* is attained through a harmonious combination of ritual action *(karma)*, knowledge *(jñāna)* and love of God *(bhakti)*. The performance of Vedic rituals for the purpose of pleasing God purifies the mind and readies it for knowledge. Knowledge leads to an understanding of one's dependence on and inseparability from God, and this awakens love and surrender toward God. Rāmānuja expanded the corpus of the *prasthāna trayi* and drew from the Vaiṣṇava *Pāñcarātras,* as well as the Tamil compositions of the Alvars.

The tradition of inquiring into, interpreting, and understanding the scripture continues today. The *Upaniṣads* with their commentaries *(bhāṣya)* and subcommentaries *(ṭīkā, vārttika),* the *Brahmasūtra*, the *Bhagavadgītā*, and independent treatises *(prakaraṇas)* expounding the standpoint of a specific school are taught and analyzed at monastic institutions *(maṭhas/mutts)* founded by different groups. Śaṅkara is credited with having founded four institutions in the four quarters of India: Śārada Mutt at Śṛṅgeri (Karnataka), Kālikā Mutt at Dvārakā (Gujarat), Jyotir Mutt at Badrinath (Uttar Pradesh), and Goverdhana Mutt at Puri (Orissa). There is a fifth Mutt at Kāñcīpuram in Tamilnadu, known as the Kāmakoṭi Mutt, which also traces its foundation to Śaṅkara. The heads of these monastries, who carry the title of Śaṅkarācārya, are influential spokespersons and symbols of the Hindu tradition. They maintain traditional schools *(pathaśālas)* in which Sanskrit and Vedic studies are taught. Similar institutions for other traditions have been established in various parts of India.

While inquiry into the meaning of the scripture, especially the *prasthāna trayi,* was the traditional preserve of the renunciant *(saṃnyāsi)*, recent developments have made the study of these texts available to interested laypeople. Several figures in the nineteenth century made significant contributions to this process. One of the earliest was Ram Mohan Roy (1774-1833). In response to missionary criticism, Ram Mohan Roy argued that the present degeneration of Hinduism was the result of reliance on texts like the *Pūranas* and *Tantras*. The *Upaniṣads*, claimed Roy, were the original revealed texts of Hinduism, and these taught a doctrine of uncomprising monotheism. He asserted the supremacy of the Vedas as *śruti* over all other texts and translated the *Upaniṣads* into Bengali and English in order to make them accessible and to disseminate their teachings. In 1828 Roy founded the Brahmo Sabha to propagate his ideals. Its services were open to all and included Vedic chanting and sermons from the *Upaniṣads*. Julius Lipner credits Roy with "restoring the Vedas to public consciousness in modern India, both as an object of study and as a source of religious inspiration."[24]

Another figure in the nineteenth century who played a prominent role in highlighting the Vedas as the authoritative scripture of Hinduism was Swami Vivekananda (1863-1902). He was a member of the Brahmo Samaj and later became the chief disciple of the Bengali mystic Ramakrishna (1836-86). Vivekananda represented Hinduism at the 1893 Parliament of Religions in Chicago. He later traveled through the United States and Europe and founded the Ramakrishna Mission in Calcutta. In his speeches in India Vivekananda frequently spoke and quoted from the *Upaniṣads*.[25] Today the Ramakrishna Mission has branches throughout India and in various parts of the world where monks regularly teach and interpret the scriptures for the lay community. The Mission runs a vigorous publishing enterprise and has translated Hindu scriptures and commentaries into English and the regional languages of India. Swami Dayananda Sarasvati, founder of the Arya Samaj, was another person in the nineteenth century who contributed to the restoration of the authority of the Vedas, and I have already commented on his work.

There are several contemporary teachers and movements who continue to contribute to the legacy of making the scriptures accessible. Swami Chinmayananda (1916-93) was the inspiration for the foundation of the Chinmaya Mission in 1953. His ministry was one of public teaching of the *Upaniṣads* and the *Bhagavadgītā*, as interpreted by Śaṅkara, in the major cities of India and abroad. He has published commentaries on these and other texs of the Vedānta tradition, as well as independent works. Over two hundred teachers affiliated with the Chinmaya Mission now work in various centers throughout the world. Swami Dayananda Sarasvati, a disciple of Swami Chinmayananda, founded the Arsha Vidya Pitham, with centers in India at Rishikesh and Coimbatore and in the United States at Saylorsburg, Pennsylvania, for study of the Vedas in the tradition of Śaṅkara. Through public lectures, youth camps, weekend retreats, summer programs, home-study courses, and audio and video tapes, many organizations are encouraging the study of the scriptures.

While there is growing public awareness of the *prasthāna trayi* and increasing opportunities for the study of these texts, the Hindu masses have always experienced *smṛti* texts in various public presentations. This may be amply illustrated by a brief survey of the variety of forms in which the *Rāmacaritamānas* of Tulasīdāsa, the most popular version of the *Rāmāyaṇa* in North India, is encountered.

THE *Rāmāyaṇa* AS *Līlā* (PLAY)

Each year, during the month of Ashvin (October/November), town dwellers and villagers throughout North India gather in open spaces to witness and to participate in the dramatic reenactment of the story of Rāma. Popularly referred to as the *Rāmlīlā* (play of Rāma), these performances last anywhere from nine to thirty days and, depending on the resources of the town or village, may include elaborate costumes and props or be a quite modest affair. Most of these performances follow the story line of the Tulasīdāsa text, which is sung throughout the drama. Through the *Rāmlīlā* festival millions of Hindus annually experience the text as drama and hear its recitation. They are able to memorize and recall its verses without ever reading the text.[26]

The *Rāmāyaṇa* as *Kathā*

The *Rāmacaritamānas* of Tulasīdāsa is also as experienced as *kathā*, a "slow systematic storytelling recitation, interspersed with prose explanations, elaborations and homely illustrations of spiritual points."[27] This tradition of expounding the sacred texts has a long history, which some sources trace to the poet Tulasīdāsa himself. The expounder *(kathāvācak)* is referred to as the *vyāsa*, a title that links the person with Vedavyāsa, who is credited with the compilation of the four Vedas. A typical *kathā* may last for several hours and usually includes *bhajans* (hymns) and *kirtan* (chanting of the names of Rāma). *Kathās* conclude with *ārtī*, the waving of oil lamps before the icon of the deity. *Kathās* continue to enjoy great popularity in India and prominent *vyāsas* can attract audiences in the thousands.

The *kathā* tradition is also alive in many parts of the Hindu diaspora, such as the Caribbean, Mauritius, and South Africa. Tulasīdāsa wrote his text in rhyming verses, and this allows for a variety of styles of singing that capture the mood of the story in its various phases. There is little doubt that many attend *kathās* for the musical experience of the text as well as for the exegesis offered by the *vyāsa*. Many popular Hindi singers such as Mukesh and Anup Jalota have recorded versions of the *Rāmacaritamānas*, and these are listened to on a daily basis in Hindu homes.

Kathās must be distinguished from a simple reading or singing of the text, which is properly referred to as a *pāṭha*. A reader or reciter *(pāṭhaka)* does not offer a commentary or exegesis of the text. *Pāṭhas* of different texts are still regularly done in homes and public places and, depending on the text selected, may run for a day or several days.

Rāmāyaṇa as Television Drama

In 1987 India's national television network, *Doordarshan*, launched a weekly serialization of the *Rāmāyaṇa*. This was the first television serializing of a sacred text. The producer and director was Ramanand Sagar, a Bombay filmmaker. Each episode was forty-five minutes in length, and the series ran for seventy-eight episodes. This series turned out to be the most popular event in the history of Indian television. The audience was estimated to be over one hundred million, and much of the country came to a standstill during the broadcast on Sunday mornings, testifying to the undiminished popularity of the *Rāmāyaṇa*. It is reported that cabinet meetings, railway schedules, and weddings were rearranged in order to accommodate the broadcasts.[28] Lutgendorf attributes the success of the series to the fact that it integrated many features drawn from the *līlā* and *kathā* traditions.[29] The *Mahābhārata* has also been serialized in ninety-three weekly episodes. Video recordings of these serials are available for sale throughout the world and are part of the prized collection in many Hindu homes.

The television drama evoked religious responses not unlike those experienced at *līlās* and *kathās*. Television sets were garlanded, *ārtī* performed for the actors and actresses, and *prasād* distributed at the end of each episode, as it would be at the end of a traditional Hindu worship service. While one may argue that these productions represent a creative use of contemporary technology to disseminate a sacred text, the story was a reconstruction drawing on a variety of ancient sources with which great liberties were taken. Many young Hindus may learn and experience the text only through this medium, and the celluloid scripture will replace the text that is traditionally heard, and chanted. The impact of this remains to be seen and assessed.

The Hindu Society of Minnesota recently added Vedic chanting to some of its regular Sunday morning worship sessions. One Sunday morning, just before the chanting commenced, a member of the audience asked one of the reciters for an explanation of the meaning of the Sanskrit hymn he was about to chant. Surprised by the question, the chanter confessed his inability to explain the meaning of the chant, but added that the meaning was not important to him. The chanting produced an experience that was its own value. One of the chanters, however, had with him a rather dense translation of the *Puruṣasūkta* from *Ṛg* Veda, which he read.

The desire on the part of the questioner not only to hear but to understand the text is perhaps a pointer to what may be an increasing need among a new generation of Hindus. While being appreciative of the significance and beauty of scriptural recitation, a generation which is less emotionally bound to the sanctity of Sanskrit will increasingly inquire about the meaning of what is recited and its relevance to day-to-day life. Such seekers would have the approval of Manu (12.103). Increasingly, ritual manuals are being published with translations and explanations of the ancient *mantras*.

The growth of literacy; the breakdown of the caste system; the translation, printing, and distribution of literature about the scriptures; and the efforts of modern Hindu movements will encourage the reading of scriptural texts by Hindus. Such a development will not make the traditional *guru*, as expounder of the text, redundant, but lay Hindus will become more actively involved in interpreting the meaning of the scriptures. Hindus will continue to hear the texts, although probably less so than in earlier times. Many more will read the texts, although few will do so in Sanskrit. The written text will grow in importance.

The acknowledgment of the authority of the Vedas as the supreme revealed texts did not curb the proliferation of other authoritative scriptural sources. These sought legitimation from the Vedas even while offering new insights and responding to different challenges. In a similar way—though scriptures of all kinds will continue to play a significant role in the religious lives of Hindus—they will not be used or experienced only in ways that simply mirror the past.

Suggested Reading

Coward, Harold. *Sacred Word and Sacred Text: Scripture in World Religions*. Maryknoll, N.Y.: Orbis Books, 1988.

O'Flaherty, Wendy Doniger. *Textual Sources for the Study of Hinduism*. New Jersey: Barnes and Noble Books, 1988.

Hawley, John Stratton, and Mark Juergensmeyer. *Songs of the Saints of India*. New York: Oxford University Press, 1988.

Lutgendorf, Phillip. *The Life of a Text: Performing the Rāmacaritmānas of Tulsidas*. Berkeley and Los Angeles: University of California Press, 1991.

Rambachan, Anantanand. *Accomplishing the Accomplished: The Vedas as a Source of Valid Knowledge in Śaṅkara*. Honolulu: University of Hawaii Press, 1991.

Notes

[1] *hari ananta hari kathā anantā*
ka"a"iṁ sunahiṁ bahu bidhi saba santā

[2] Klaus K. Klostermaier, *A Survey of Hinduism* (Albany, N.Y.: State University of New York Press, 1994), 65.

[3] See *Upaniṣads,* trans. Patrick Olivelle (Oxford: Oxford University Press, 1996), 156-57.

[4] Ibid., 2.4.1-4, p. 28.

[5] Various Hindu traditions differ in their claims about the nature of the self, the absolute, the world, and the relationship among these three.

[6] Harold Coward, *Sacred Word and Sacred Text: Scripture in World Religions* (Maryknoll, N.Y.: Orbis Books, 1988), 107.

[7] There are exceptional cases of liberated persons who are reborn for the specific purpose of serving humanity. They are referred to as *ādhikārika puruṣas* and are not subject to ignorance.

[8] Dates are only approximate and differ considerably from scholar to scholar.

[9] See, for example, Swami Prabhavnanda, *The Spiritual Heritage of India* (California: Vedanta Press, 1979), 34-35, who cites the *Ṛg* Veda text, *ekaṁ sat viprā bahudhā Vadanti* ("reality is one; sages call it by many names"), to explain that the deities are many expressions of one God.

[10] For a good discussion of this issue see Klostermaier, *A Survey of Hinduism*, chap. 8, Klostermaier uses the term *polydevatāism* instead of *polytheism.*

[11] See Ganganatha Jha, trans, *The Pūrva Mīmāmsa-Sūtras of Jaimini* (Varanasi: Bharatiya Publishing House, 1979).

[12] See Swami Gambhirananda, trans., *The Brahma-sūtra Bhāṣya of Śaṅkarācārya* (Calcutta: Advaita Ashrama, 1977), 1.3.28.

[13] For a concise summary of various Hindu views on the nature of language see Coward, *Sacred Word and Sacred Text*, 111-16.

[14] *sargaśca pratisargaśca vaṁśo manvantarāṇi ca*
vaṁśānucaritaṁ cāpi purāṇam pañca lakṣaṇam

[15] For a good discussion of the work of the North India poet-saints, see John Stratton Hawley and Mark Juergensmeyer, *Songs of the Saints of India* (New York: Oxford University Press, 1988).

[16] See Coward, *Sacred Word and Sacred Text*, 120-22.

[17] The *Gāyatrī mantra* (*Ṛg* Veda 3.62.10) is as follows:
Aum bhūr bhuvassvaḥ
tat saviturvareṇyam

bhargo devasya dhimahi
dhiyo yo naḥ pracodayāt
Aum, the Lord, is the one who is most worshipful. We meditate on that all-knowing Lord. May he set our intellects in the right direction.

[18] For a concise introduction to the nature and use of *mantras* in Hindu daily life, see Harold Coward and David Goa, *Mantra: Hearing the Divine in India* (Pennsylvania: Anima Books, 1991).

[19] See *Bhagavadgītā* 8:5.

[20] *The Laws of Manu*, trans. G. Buhler, Sacred Books of the East, vol. 25 (Delhi: Motilal Banarsidass, 1988 reprint), 12:103.

[21] The six orthodox schools that accept the authority of the Vedas are *Nyāya, Vaiśeṣika, Sāṁkhya, Yoga, Pūrva Mīmāṁsā,* and *Vedānta.* Jainism, Buddhism, and Cāravākas are regarded as nonorthodox. Each of the six orthodox schools has an authoritative *sūtra* text that enunciates its worldview. The term *sūtra* means "thread," and a *sūtra* text consists of a collection of brief statements summarizing the teachings of a particular school. The style is aphoristic and commentaries are required for clarification.

[22] The *sūtras* of Jaimini (ca. 200 B.C.E.) are the earliest systematic work of this tradition. Jaimini's work was commented upon by Śabarasvāmin (ca. 200 C.E.), and the latter's work was commented upon by Prabhākara and Kumārila Bhaṭṭa. The two Mīmāṁsā schools are named after Prabhākara and Bhaṭṭa.

[23] For a detailed discussion of Śaṅkara's rationale for the authority of the Vedas, see Anantanand Rambachan, *Accomplishing the Accomplished: The Vedas as a Source of Valid Knowledge in Śaṅkara* (Honolulu: University of Hawaii Press, 1991).

[24] Julius Lipner, *Hindus: Their Religious Beliefs and Practices* (London: Routledge, 1994), 66.

[25] For a detailed treatment of the attitude to scripture of Ram Mohan Roy and Vivekananda, see Anantanand Rambachan, *The Limits of Scripture: Vivekananda's Reinterpretation of the Vedas* (Honolulu: University of Hawaii Press, 1994).

[26] See Philip Lutgendorf, *The Life of a Text: Performing the Rāmacaritmānas of Tulsidas* (Berkeley and Los Angeles: University of California Press, 1991), chap. 5.

[27] Ibid., 115.

[28] Lipner, *Hindus: Their Religious Practices and Beliefs,* 142.

[29] Ibid., 411-12.

5

Sikhism

Harjot Oberoi

The holy book is the abode of the Lord (pothi paramesar ka than).
—Guru Arjan (1563-1606)

I would like to begin with a personal narrative. In mid-1987 I accepted a faculty position at the University of British Columbia; I was appointed chair of Punjabi language, literature, and Sikh Studies. I had the privilege of serving in this position for ten years, and from this period in my teaching career I could narrate many an episode that would richly illustrate the topic of this study. But from all of my recollections, one stands out and is perhaps the most apt one to introduce the topic of sacred word and sacred text in the Sikh religion. One spring afternoon I heard a knock on my office door. My visitor was a young Sikh student, whom I had never met before. He was about twenty-two years or so in age, elegantly dressed, wore an impressive green turban, and had a long beard. We exchanged greetings, and I welcomed him into my office. As we sat down to talk, I asked what brought him to see me. He mentioned that recently he had visited our Asian Studies library, and while browsing through the racks, which were crowded with books in vernacular literatures, he was shocked to find a copy of the primary Sikh scripture, reverently known as the *Sri Guru Granth Sahib*, on the shelves. His point was simple and powerful. How could the library staff be so insensitive as to place the Sikh sacred text alongside the mundane and the profane. The Sikh holy book was not simply some reference work, a book among other books, a volume of paper and ink. It occupied the most honored place in the minds and hearts of Sikhs. This was a repository of deep mysteries and sacred utterances. Ordinarily it was found high on a lectern, either in a Sikh shrine or a household, wrapped in expensive silks and devotional coverings, and treated with utmost dignity and respect.

One part of me instinctively knew that what this student was protesting was indeed true. Our secular world, and one of its most cherished institutions, the academy, does not know how to treat sacred writings. But my internal reflections were not going to help in the matter at hand. So I promptly started an exercise in some gentle reasoning with this student. I proposed two things to him. First, the library treated the sacred writings of all religions with great respect; besides the Sikh holy book we also had acquired the texts of the other faith traditions. Thus our professional staff did not imply any disrespect by displaying the primary Sikh scripture. Second, given that Sikhism was now viewed as a world religion, it was important that all major libraries possess a copy of the Sikh scripture. This would allow all those who were interested in the affairs of the Sikhs readily to consult their most valuable resource. My reasoning did not have much of an impact on the student, and he looked rather dissatisfied. Somewhat defeatedly, I proposed that he come in a day or two and we could resume our conversation. Meanwhile, I called a colleague of mine, Mr. Inderjit Singh Bhugra, our Indic librarian, and sought his advice. He immediately proposed that I send this student over to him, which I did. When I next spoke to Mr. Bhugra, he said the matter had been resolved. Naturally, I asked him what was his solution. He said he simply recounted to the student his days as a librarian at the Punjabi University, in Patiala. This university is a premier institution of higher education in the homeland of the Sikhs. And the library of course displayed copies of the *Sri Guru Granth Sahib* on its shelves. But to show all of the requisite respect, the library bindings of the scripture were in two split-volumes. This separated and distinguished the university holding from the regular, unsplit editions of the scripture. It was an uneasy compromise, but clearly it had worked well for all these years. Following that Punjab convention, our university library too displayed the two-volume edition. When the student heard this account from a Canadian librarian who also happened to be a Sikh, he was finally satisfied that no disrespect was meant.

Allow me now to place this story in the context of the evolution of the Sikh faith. For, given our secular moorings, the deeper layers of this library narrative cannot be understood without coming to terms with the totality of Sikh self-experience, history, and theology. Although in the beginning Sikhism was a regional movement based in northern India, today it has acquired a global presence. We find Sikh communities virtually in all parts of the world. While in some countries, like Canada, the United States, and England, the Sikh population is substantial, in other countries, like France, Australia, and Argentina, there is a small Sikh population.[1] To find Sikhs all over the world is quite amazing considering that the total Sikh population is no more than twenty million. Even within India Sikhs are only 2 percent of the total population of 980 million. Despite these small numbers one finds Sikhs all over the subcontinent. All major Indian cities have several Sikh centers of congregation, known as *gurdwaras;* their constituents engage in a variety of professions and businesses. But wherever one may find Sikhs, their origins are closely tied to an area of northern India known as the Punjab (five-waters). Almost all Sikhs identify with the Punjab as their homeland, except for a small group of Caucasians who have in the recent past converted to Sikhism. What then is Sikhism?

THE "FORGOTTEN TRADITION"

Exactly two decades ago a well-known sociologist of religion, Mark Juergensmeyer, published an influential paper entitled "The Forgotten Tradition: Sikhism in the Study of World Religions."[2] In this essay he argued that scholars of comparative religion had either simply ignored the Sikh tradition, or if they noticed it all, they merely presented it in a few sentences as a synthesis of Hinduism and Islam. Fortunately, in the intervening years the situation has improved considerably. Texts on world religions now include sophisticated accounts of the Sikh faith and the simplistic rendering of Sikhism as a fusion of Islam and Hinduism has virtually disappeared. Instead, it is being increasingly recognized that Sikhism is rooted in a particular religious experience, piety, and culture and informed by a unique inner revelation, initially carried and exemplified in the life and teachings of its founder, Guru Nanak.[3]

Guru Nanak was born in a village not far from the modern city of Lahore in 1469 C.E.—three years after the publication of the Gutenberg Bible and fourteen years before the birth of Martin Luther (1483-1546). Globally this was a period of intense change, critical reflections, and technological advances. Based on a vast corpus of biographical literature described as the *janamsakhis* by the Sikhs we can divide Guru Nanak's life into three distinct phases: his early contemplative life, the enlightenment experience accompanied by extensive travels, and a foundational climax that resulted in the establishment and gathering of the first Sikh community.[4] It is worthwhile to report some key anecdotes from each of these life stages in order to gain a glimpse into how Nanak came to be viewed as a Guru or inspired teacher by an incipient community in the Punjab. From the hagiographic literature we know that Nanak was a precocious child. His father, Kalu, wished his son to be a herdsman or an accountant. But Nanak was not keen on pursuing paternal dreams. One day the father, determined to instruct young Nanak in a profession, gave him a large amount of money and asked him to go invest it in some lucrative venture in a neighboring town. With much hesitation Nanak agreed to the journey. He had barely stepped out of the village when he came across a group of traveling mendicants who had not eaten for days. Perturbed by their hunger, Nanak instantly decided that there could be no better investment of his funds than feeding a group of holy men. So he immediately proceeded to the neighboring town, procured a large supply of rations and groceries, and returned to feed his new friends. The holy men, greatly pleased by the services and generosity of the young man, blessed him and went their way. When Nanak returned home that evening and reported on the day's transactions, his father, to put it mildly, was not impressed. Finally, when it dawned on the family that Nanak would not be turning into a businessman, it was arranged that he find employment with the city of Sultanpur.

Although Nanak worked at his job diligently, early each morning and late each evening he spent long hours in meditation and devotional singing. One early morning while he was bathing in the city river he disappeared without leaving a trace. Family members and the civic authorities searched frantically but failed to find him. It was widely feared that he had drowned. Three days later he was discovered, and as he stepped out of the water, his first words were: "There is no Hindu, there is no Muslim." This certainly was a profound statement in the context of the religious culture of medieval Punjab. The two dominant religions of the region were Islam and Hinduism. Nanak seemed to be discounting both. He was now ready to proclaim a radically new vision. In Sikh self-understanding, the three days that Nanak had disappeared are viewed as his attainment of enlightenment. During these seventy-two hours he is said to have had an audience with God and to have been sent back urgently to start a new religion. The powerful symbolism of a three-day absence and immersion in water serves as a wonderful metaphor of dissolution, transformation, and spiritual perfection. In 1496 Nanak launched a new community or what in Sikh vocabulary is simply described as the *panth*. Those who joined the new panth, acknowledged Nanak as their Guru.

Guru Nanak was now twenty-seven years of age; he had been married for approximately a decade and was father to two young sons. In the following years Nanak traveled extensively. According to the hagiographic narratives the Guru undertook extensive and hazardous journeys in each of the four directions of the compass. He proceeded as far as Assam in the east and Mecca in the West. During these tours he composed and recited spiritual poetry, sought out Hindu and Muslim religious figures, particularly at famous centers of pilgrimage like Banaras and Baghdad, and engaged them in critical debate on the nature of truth, value of ritual and pilgrimage, role of external religious authority, and means of deliverance. After having spent twenty-four years in travel and itinerant preaching, Nanak finally returned to his native Punjab in 1519 and established a vibrant religious community at Kartarpur. Here, for a period of twenty years, he taught his disciples, old and new, the art of meditation and right conduct through two key spiritual practices: *nam-simran* (remembrance of the divine name) and *kirtan* (singing hymns of praise).

What was the nature of divinity in Guru Nanak's theology? Although it would be easy to answer this question by simply invoking the vocabulary of Abrahamic monotheism, that would fail to do justice to the full range of meanings and associations that Nanak reserved for God. He conceived of a Supreme Being who is eternal, infinite, and all-pervasive; self-existent; and a perennial source of well-being, compassion, grace, and love. This Akal Purakh, the name that Nanak often used for God, is beyond time. He is the creator, without fear and devoid of enmity. Paradoxically, he is both *nirguna* and *saguna;* that is, this Supreme Being both possesses attributes and is without attributes. And yet he is formless and cannot be contained in an image. The Akal Purakh responds to the devotion of all his followers without distinctions of caste or gender. Nanak instructed his followers that the central objective of human life was *mukti,* or release. Human life entailed sorrow and *samsara*—the constant cycle of birth, death, and rebirth. Release from bondage, self-delusion, and the cycle of transmigration could be had by concentrating on God's Name. Those who succeeded in attaining this goal would share two attributes. First, they would experience *vismad,* or ever-growing wonder. Second, they would attain *sahaj,* or total equanimity. Thus the cycle of transmigration and resulting afflictions is broken.

Guru Nanak's spiritual message found an institutional expression through four key institutions: *dharamsals*, *sangat*, *langar,* and *guruship*. The term *dharamsal* is derived from Sanskrit and originally meant "court of justice or tribunal." By Nanak's time it was used in the vernacular for a charitable place of rest. During the Guru's frequent journeys Sikhs would commonly gather in a *dharamsal* to worship the Akal Purakh and sing devotional hymns. In time, these congregational spots turned into regular and much frequented centers of Sikh religious culture. All of the Sikhs who gathered together for worship came to be described as *sangat*. This term, implying association or company, turned into a key sociological factor in the expansion and regional organization of Sikhism. At the same time, it expressed a doctrinal content similar to the Buddhist *sangha* or the Muslim *umma*. The third communal institution launched by Guru Nanak was that of *langar*, or public kitchen. In part to negate the social distinctions of medieval Indian society, and in part to enhance social solidarity within an embryonic community, Nanak asked his disciples to sit and dine together. Soon this became a major symbol of Sikh religious practices and self-definition. Finally, before his death Nanak chose a successor, also called a Guru, thus launching a spiritual lineage that was to continue for almost 170 years. Between 1539 and 1708 there were nine successor Gurus, and each one greatly contributed to the task of consolidating and institutionalizing Sikhism.[5]

For our purposes it is important to note four key additions to the rapidly evolving structure of early Sikh tradition. The fourth Guru, Ram Das (1534-81), acquired a large parcel of land and founded the future city of Amritsar. Much of the civilizational idiom associated with Sikhism was to emerge out of this city. This was the site where the fifth Guru, Arjan (1563-1606), chose to construct the famous Sikh shrine called the Harimandir, today popularly known as the Golden Temple.[6] It was also Arjan who took definitive steps toward compiling the writings of his four predecessors, his own work, and a large corpus of other poet-saints into a scripture that scholars frequently call the *Adi-Granth,* but that Sikhs out of deference address as the *Sri Guru Granth Sahib*. He completed this crucial and enormous task in a two-year period from 1603 to 1604. Once completed, the *Granth Sahib* was installed in the newly constructed Harimandir shrine. We shall, of course, discuss this sacred text in more detail below.

Some of the most visible symbols associated with Sikhism were endowed during the tenure of the tenth Guru, Gobind Singh (1666-1708).[7] The Khalsa component of Sikhism was his contribution.[8] Let me briefly explain what the Khalsa is. The word is of Arabic origin and is commonly understood to denote purity. During Gobind Singh's time it was also used in the lexicon of the Mughal imperial authority to denote all those lands that were directly owned and administered by the crown instead of the state treasury. Following Mughal usage, when Gobind Singh employed the term he was speaking of all those Sikhs who directly related to the office of the Guru, without the intervention of any "priestly" intermediaries. At least from the time of the third Guru there had emerged within the Sikh movement a sector of people who can be classed, if not as "priestly" intermediaries, then certainly as ritual specialists who stood between the Master and the lay public. The tenth Guru believed that the system had outlived its purpose and some of the ritual specialists called *masands* had turned corrupt. In 1699 he called for an end to the office of the *masands* by launching the Khalsa order. In addition to the fact that all Sikhs could now directly relate to him without first having to go to the *masands*, they were now also expected to be initiated into a new religious discipline. While describing the regime of this discipline would take us beyond the scope of this chapter, it will be useful to state at least one prominent aspect of this new order. All males initiated into the Khalsa were expected to uphold five dress marks. Since all these five items begin with the Punjabi letter *k*, collectively they are referred to as *panj kakke*. They are *kes* (uncut hair), *kangha* (a comb worn in the hair), *kirpan* (a sword), *kara* (a steel bangle), and *kachh* (shorts).[9] Equally significant was Gobind Singh's decision to end the line of personal Guruship. For the future he endowed the Sikh holy scripture, the *Granth Sahib*, as the Guru. This was a decision of great theological and historical significance. The *Granth Sahib* came to be acknowledged as the manifestation of divine revelation as brought forth to the world in the writings of the Sikh Gurus. Behind this formal recognition of the scripture as Guru was a doctrine that had been emerging from the time of Guru Nanak. All of the Gurus in their respective compositions repeatedly made the point that the node of transmission between the Akal Purakh and humanity was *bani*, or divine utterance. And since the *Granth Sahib* was the most concrete representation of this *bani*, Gobind Singh declared it to be the future Guru. Starting in the eighteenth century, the Sikh prayer called *ardas* came to be concluded with the following exhortation:

> From the Timeless One there came the
> command,

> In accordance with which was established the Panth.
> To all Sikhs there comes this order:
> Acknowledge as Guru the Granth,
> Acknowledge the Granth as Guru,
> For it is the manifest body of the Masters.
> Those who seek union with the Supreme Being,
> Seek him in the Word!
> The Khalsa shall rule,
> No enemy shall remain.
> All who endure suffering and pain
> Shall be brought to the safety of the Guru's protection.

We have reached a point in our discussion where we cannot go any further in our deliberations without having some preliminary idea about the structure, organization, and content of the Sikh holy book.

THE STRUCTURE AND LANGUAGE OF THE *GURU GRANTH SAHIB*

The Sikh holy book is a substantial work, with 1430 printed pages in large format. While a layperson may find the architecture of the text rather overwhelming, familiarity with a few organizational principles can provide relatively easy access to the richness of its contents. Unlike the Abrahamic scriptures, the *Guru Granth Sahib* is not a work of genealogy, history, or social code. Essentially in its detail it is a work of religious hymns, where considerable attention has been given to play of metaphors, poetical meter, and rules of oral transmission. The whole work is divided into three key sections: a brief introductory section made up of liturgical readings, a large middle portion, and an epilogue. The first part opens with a very well-known composition of Guru Nanak known as *Japji* and then goes on to list several other readings that a devout Sikh will recite or sing on three occasions during the day: early morning, sunset, and before going to bed. The central part of the scripture, where the bulk of the writings of the Sikh Gurus is lodged, is ordered around thirty-one *ragas,* or Indian musical notations. For instance, under *raga* Gujri we find the writings of Gurus Nanak, Amardas, Ramdas, and Arjan, and of the poet-saints Kabir, Namdev, and Ravidas. Thus what was important in the formatting of the scripture was not so much chapter or page as musical mode. In a structural sense, therefore, the holy book was originally meant primarily for collective chanting, singing, and recitation rather than for personal reading. The final part of the scripture consists of a series of miscellaneous works, like the compositions of professional musicians patronized by Guru Arjan or the *raga-mala* or list of *ragas*, pieces that could not be easily accommodated within the musical settings of the middle part.

Scholars have long debated how precisely to characterize the language of the *Adi-Granth*. The early view was that it was made up of several dialects and a wide variety of linguistic usage. This theory has recently been put aside, and it is now proposed that the language of the holy book is simply the linguistic code prevalent in fifteenth- and sixteenth-century Punjab, which was informed by Punjabi, Hindi, and Persian. A well-known scholar of Sikh affairs, W. H. McLeod, gave this linguistic formation the handy name of Sant Bhasha, or the language of saints.[10] More recently another scholar, Christopher Shackle, called it the sacred language of the Sikhs.[11] And this latter characterization seems to be apt. For Sikhs tend to treat not only the text as holy but also the language that it is written in. The script in which the *Guru Granth Sahib* is written is called Gurmukhi, meaning what has come from the mouth of the Guru. And indeed it is firm Sikh belief that the Gurmukhi alphabet was invented by the second Sikh Guru. Thus, much like the Hindus who treat Sanskrit as a sacred language, and Muslims who consider Arabic in a similar light, the Sikhs too endow Gurmukhi with a similar reverence.

In concluding this section, I would like to list a few samples from the writings of the Sikh Gurus and other poet-saints included in the scripture:

> For millions of years there was nothing but darkness over the void. There was neither earth nor sky, only the Infinite Will.
> There was neither night nor day, sun nor moon, and the Lord was in a state of trance.
> The sources of creation did not exist, there was no speech, no air, no water, no birth, no death, no coming or going, no regions, no seven seas, no worlds above or below.
> The trinity of Brahma, Vishnu, and Shiva did not exist. There was no other only the one Absolute Lord.[12]

Another passage:

> The Infinite Lord has enshrined his might within all.
> He himself is detached and without limit or equal.
> He created nature and inanimate nature came from the existing void. From his own Being came air, water and the world, bodies and his spirit within them.
> Your light, O Lord is within fire, water and living beings and in your Absolute self lies the power of creation.
> From the Absolute Lord emanated Brahma, Vishnu, and Shiva: from him came all the ages...
> All that springs from the Lord merges with him again.
> By his play the Lord has created nature and by his word has manifested the wonder.
> From himself he has made day and night.
> From him came creation and destruction, pleasure and pain.
> The godly minded remain stable and detached from the effects of good or ill and find their home in God.[13]

THE POWER OF THE REVEALED WORD IN THE SIKH TRADITION

It is becoming increasingly commonplace to examine the oral experience of a scripture within religious communities.[14] Of late, the elevated status of the printed word in our culture has come under increasing scrutiny, and it has been suggested that we have lost a rich heritage by not staying attuned with orality, particularly as it was experienced in the sacred realm. William Graham states this revisionist viewpoint most forcefully:

> Reading for us today is a silent, apparently wholly mental process. Our implicit model of written literature is the mode of communication to a silent reader through the eye alone, from a definitive written text. We assume that reading is simply mental cognition of visual symbols on a page. Our usual training in reading, especially that in speed-reading, is aimed at ridding us of vocalization and even subvocalization....There is, however, much to be said for the contention that, whether we recognize it or not, reading is an oral process: reading a text means converting it to sound, aloud, subvocally, or in the imagination, syllable-by-syllable in slow reading or sketchily in the rapid reading common to high-technology cultures. Oral speech remains the intrinsic form of human communication, and for most literate peoples of history outside our own society in recent times, reading has normally been a vocal, physical activity, even for the solitary reader. One normally "mouthed" the words of the text and preferably voiced them aloud, not only in reading them but even in composing or copying them into writing.[15]

Sikh tradition closely shares this sentiment expressed by Graham. The devotees who gathered around Guru Nanak, the founder of the faith, were often instructed in the oral recitation of the *bani*. For, in Sikh theology, the divine utterance was the principal mode of revelation. And human salvation was only possible by memorizing, reciting, and mastering the sacred word.

The centrality of the revealed word is repeatedly asserted in the *Adi-Granth*, as will become clear from the following quotations from the Sikh scripture:

> (i) Man is born and then dies. Where did he come from? Say where did he emerge and where does he go? How is he bound to transmigration and how is he released? How may he merge with the eternal Lord? He who has the Lord's word in his heart and on his tongue transcends desire. Man comes and goes because of desire. The godly are free for they are immersed in his Name and dwell on the Word.[16]
>
> (ii) Nanak, the supreme Lord, the true Creator, is known by means of the Word.[17]
>
> (iii) By prayer I live, without it I die. The name of the True one is hard to say. [18]

From very early on, in the Sikh tradition, recitation of the sacred word became an integral part of a devotee's daily life. The fourth Guru, Ram Das, turned this belief into a liturgical practice. He prescribed a routine for members of the community that included rising early in the morning, bathing, and then reciting the sacred compositions from memory. It is worth citing this hymn, for it has come to influence profoundly Sikh interaction with the sacred word:

> He who calls himself a Sikh of the true Guru, he should get up in the early hours of the morning and recite the Name of God. He should make effort to rise before dawn and take a bath. By repeating the Lord's Name, under the guidance of the Guru, all his troubles will end and all his blemishes will be destroyed. Then when the day dawns, he should sing the *bani* of the Guru and remember the name of the Supreme Being while sitting or moving. He who remembers my Lord with every breath and loaf, that *Gursikh* is dear to the Guru. He on whom my Lord showers His Blessings, the Guru instructs that *Gursikh*. I beg for the dust of the feet of that *Gursikh*, who not only recites the Word of God but also makes others to repeat it.[19]

In this hymn memorization and recitation of the sacred word are woven into the very definition of being a Sikh. Those who were unable to recite and perform the liturgical requirements were not to be taken seriously by the Guru and the subsequent tradition. This has been a constant factor in the ritual life of the community for over five hundred years. From one end of the Sikh world to another the individual and corporate life within the community revolves around capturing the power of the sacred word. We get a taste of this liturgical imperative in a recent autobiography by a Sikh in the diaspora. Tara Singh Bains, an ex-soldier from the Indian army, immigrated to Canada in the early 1950s. He records the following episode from his childhood:

> Father told me to memorize the morning prayer, the Japji Sahib, composed by Guru Nanak, our First Guru. It has thirty-eight verses and takes twenty minutes to recite. It was the only verse from the holy scriptures that I learned by heart before I became an independent person. Father made me do it; he ordered it; but it was a good thing. Sikhism was all around me.[20]

A similar anecdote could be narrated by a great majority of those who belong to the Sikh tradition. Either from childhood on or at some later stage all Sikhs learn to recite some portion of the scripture. And many Sikh schools both in India and overseas hold regular classes to instruct young boys and girls in the art of recitation. According to the Sikh code of conduct, commonly referred to as the *Rahit-Maryada*, every Sikh has to recite a prescribed section of the *bani* three times a day. The first portion, which is to be recited early in the morning, preferably between 3 and 6 A.M., consists of the following sections of the scripture: *Japji*, *Jap*, and the *Savayyas*. This is to be followed at sunset by a reading or chanting of the *Sodar Rahiras*. And finally, before retiring for the night, a brief *Sohila* selection is to be recited.

Sikh corporate life revolves around a *gurdwara,* a Punjabi word that literally means "the door of the Guru." Technically, any place that houses a *Guru Granth Sahib* can be called a *gurdwara*, and that could include a room set aside in a Sikh house for worship purposes. But often the term is used for elaborate shrines built by community members for congregational purposes. The most famous *gurdwaras* are historical shrines that are associated with the lives of the Sikh Gurus, for instance, the world-famous Golden Temple in Amritsar. But hundreds of *gurdwaras* have been constructed in modern times in India and in all of the other places where Sikhs reside to accommodate the needs of an expanding community. To give one example from a city that I am familiar with, metropolitan Vancouver, on the west coast of Canada, has six *gurdwaras*, all of which were constructed from the late 1960s onward to provide congregational space for the diasporic community. And each one can accommodate a congregation of over two thousand Sikhs.

For the purpose of this chapter it is crucial to note three congregational activities in a *gurdwara* that center on the sacred text. First, the focus of Sikh piety and devotion in a *gurdwara* is the Sikh holy book. The scripture covered in expensive silks and supported by cushions is laid on a lectern that is covered by an elaborate canopy. When the scripture is opened and read from, it is always to be attended by a *granthi*, an official reader or a lay devotee. At the conclusion of each day's service the *Guru Granth Sahib* is transported with great respect to a resting place within the shrine for the night. Second, the *sangat* or congregation assembled in a *gurdwara* worships by singing hymns from the scripture. Often this congregational singing, called *kirtan*, is led by a trio of professional *ragis* or singers. Many *ragis* have extensive training in classical music and, depending on their vocal and instrumental skills, can attain a considerable reputation within the community. They are looked upon with great affection, and some, like the contemporary Darshan Singh Ragi, have a huge following. It is worth noting here that all of the best-known *ragis* have large collections of musical recordings that are sold in stores and may be played daily in many Sikh households. Third, the principal official or *granthi* of a *gurdwara* includes within the ritual proceedings of the day an extensive discourse that includes an exegesis of a selection from the *Guru Granth Sahib*.

Such exegetical presentations have been part of Sikh ritual life from the days of the Sikh Gurus. Since the word is seen to be a key to human salvation, interpreting, understanding, and imbibing this word in everyday life has been viewed as an integral aspect of Sikh tradition. Many of the early Sikh manuscripts are exegeses of the sacred text. The Sikh Gurus themselves are known to have widely commented and elaborated on the scripture.

Much as the scripture is central to communal worship, similarly the text is also the focus of individual piety. Most devout Sikhs begin their day with the ritual of *hukam* (the taking of a commandment) or *vak* (reciting the Guru's word). The practice begins with a person sitting behind a lectern, where the holy book is placed, and then opening the text at random and reciting aloud, often with other family members joining in, the first hymn at the top of the left-hand page. This *hukam* then becomes the order of the day. The individual who first read it, and others who may have joined in, reflect on the meanings and implication of the *hukam* for the rest of the day. It is not uncommon to have the *hukam* used as a source of inspiration to face the everyday tribulations of life. The *hukam* that is obtained early in the morning at the Golden Temple, the premier Sikh institution in Amritsar, is now posted on the World Wide Web so that Sikh congregations can receive it as a message of the Guru.

Let me now turn briefly to the question of scriptural authority within the Sikh community. Theoretically, it is not difficult to propose that the *Guru Granth Sahib* today occupies a position of supreme authority within the Sikh tradition. For to whom else would the Sikhs turn in search of answers to fundamental questions or at a time of sociopolitical crises? Hew McLeod, an eminent scholar of Sikh affairs notes:

> Sikhs have insistently been taught, in their homes and *gurdwaras*, that the scripture is infallible and if any question should arise they need only consult its sacred pages. For some a specific answer is expected, the Guru Granth Sahib being regarded essentially as a talisman. Others view the guidance of the scripture as general, the message being absorbed by the moulding of the understanding through regular daily readings.[21]

But this statement needs to be qualified in light of history and communal practices. During the eighteenth century there arose among the Sikhs the twin doctrines of Guru-Panth and Guru-Granth.[22] Under the doctrine of the Guru-Panth, the community was supreme, and under the doctrine of Guru-Granth, the scripture was supreme. This duality was easy to live with when Sikhs did not enjoy political power. But with the rise of a Sikh state in the early nineteenth century, the doctrine of Guru-Panth became hard to practice. If everyone was an equal member of the Panth, how was one to run a political state? The Sikh ruler Maharaja Ranjit Singh was astute in these matters. He gradually diluted the concept of the Guru-Panth and gave greater importance to the doctrine of Guru-Granth. This allowed the rise of a new political elite among the Sikhs. The importance of a textual Guru continued to increase even after the demise of the Sikh kingdom. As the Punjab became a part of the British Empire in the second half of the nineteenth century, there arose among the Sikhs a reform movement called the Singh Sabha. This was a Sikh effort to come to terms with the project of modernity. But modernity, as we know, is a tough equation to handle. Karl Marx once described modernity as everything solid that melts into the air. This constant flux and dissonance of modernity was handled by the Sikhs by even further enlarging the historical theology of scripture as Guru. In other words, in a world where everything was being radically transformed, many in the Sikh community desired to have at least one fixed point of reference, and this became the *Guru Granth Sahib*. Interestingly, the exegetical traditions of the book that emerged in the twentieth century sought to focus on a singular interpretation of the sacred text. While in earlier times there was considerable diversity and plurality in interpreting the sacred text, more recently the Sikh community has moved toward univocal readings. It seems that the project of modernity has built into it an imperative of uniformity. And, consciously or unconsciously, Sikh collective identity and scriptural tradition moved toward a much greater uniformity in the twentieth century. One suspects that the agents of modernization, like the printing press and educational institutions, have had a great role to play in generating this homogeneity.

AN ETHNOGRAPHY OF *RITES DE PASSAGE* AND THE SACRED TEXT

Finally, it will be worthwhile to note how the scripture is used among the Sikh for performing the key life-cycle rituals. Religion as a systematized sociological unit claiming the unbridled loyalty of its constituents can hardly be persuasive if it does not provide a powerful framework for the performance of life-cycle rites. These rites constitute a communicative grid par excellence that simultaneously transmits identity, a particular vision of history, an etiquette of interpersonal transactions, and communal solidarity. Ritual enactments thus are a condensed statement of the most deeply held values in a society. As metaphors of collective consciousness they inform of cultural boundaries; communicate notions of time, space, and sacrality; endow people with a significant sense of personal identity; and often reinforce social order. It is worth noting in passing that the meaning of the Indian term *samskara*, widely used in lay parlance to denote life-cycle rituals, is to "prepare," "refine," and to "complete."[23] In other words, these rituals (*samskaras*) have the power to distill and complete what is undistilled and incomplete in human life. In the Sikh universe the role of life-cycle rituals is further reinforced by introducing the sacred text in all of the key rites.

Let us begin by looking at the rituals surrounding the birth of a baby. Soon after the birth the infant is administered sweetened water and a recitation is made from the holy text that includes the prologue and the first five stanzas of the *Japji*, the opening composition in the *Guru Granth Sahib*. A few days later the family and the baby visit the local *gurdwara,* where a simple naming ceremony is held. The sacred text is opened at random and the name is chosen from the same letter as the first composition on the left-hand page. Thus the child is welcomed into the world with a blessing and marking from the holy book.

As the child grows up, he or she may choose to be initiated into the Khalsa order of Sikhism (there is no fixed age for this initiation). This key initiation ceremony—known as *amrit sanskar*—can only be performed in the presence of the *Guru Granth Sahib;* a collectivity of five Sikhs who are already initiated lead the ceremony. Each one of them recites aloud from a set of prescribed hymns at the ritual.[24] In short, without the intervention of the sacred sound one cannot become a Khalsa Sikh. At the conclusion of the ceremony a *hukam* is taken from the holy book.

Similarly, a Sikh marriage can only be performed in the presence of the *Guru Granth Sahib*. During the marriage rite both the bride and the bridegroom have to circumambulate the holy text four times. While they are doing so, those officiating at the wedding, often a trio of *ragis*, sing prescribed hymns from the sacred text. Once again, it is sacred sound that provides legitimacy for a key life-cycle ritual.

And finally, at the time of death, both in the period preceding the cremation and in the post-cremation rites, recourse is made to the *Guru Granth Sahib*. In the period before the cremation professional readers or members of the family continuously read from the scripture. After the cremation proceedings are over, the family normally initiates a complete reading of the *Guru Granth Sahib*. This may happen at home or in a *gurdwara*. At the conclusion of the reading, which may take anywhere from three to ten days, a *bhog* ceremony is performed.

From the theoretical and empirical materials presented in this chapter, it is easy to conceptualize how the key Sikh scripture has turned into a meta-resource for Sikh identity, cultural practices, personal piety, and collective liturgical purposes. But more than issues of identity and liturgical usages, what is unique here and draws our attention is the fact that the holy book has come to occupy the status of a "textual Guru" in the tradition. While in the history of religions it is common to document the rise of what Brian Stock once so aptly described as "textual communities," those that subscribe to the holiness of a book, the Sikh experience of having a "textual Guru" is certainly uncommon. In the Indic religious environment a Guru is generally a living person who communicates divine knowledge and aids his disciples by providing them with a cognitive map for salvation. In the Sikh religion, after the tenure of the ten living Gurus, this role has been performed by the holy book. Simply put, the Guru speaks through the book.

Allow me to narrate here one story that would illustrate the practical implications of this theological doctrine. The period of the 1920s in the history of the Punjab and the chronicles of the Sikhs was a time of intense social change and mass political mobilization. Much of this change followed as a consequence of the dislocations resulting from the First World War. As existing rules of caste hierarchy began to collapse, many outcastes saw avenues of social mobility in the egalitarian message of Sikhism. Some of these outcastes approached modern Sikh leaders to be initiated into the community. These leaders, greatly influenced by contemporary ideologies of revolution and freedom, readily agreed to the petition by outcaste groups. However, the traditional leadership of the Sikhs was not so willing to admit the outcastes into the ranks of Sikhism. And it was these traditional leaders who controlled access to one of the most eminent Sikh places of worship—the Golden Temple. The newly converted outcastes and their radical leaders wanted the initiates to go and make offerings at the Golden Temple. As was expected, the traditional leadership refused them admittance. When the controversy over this issue threatened to turn into a major disturbance, the two parties agreed to consult the textual Guru and see what guidance they would receive. The scripture, as was the practice, was opened at random and the following passage came to attention:

> Upon the worthless He bestows His grace,
> brother,
> if they will serve the true Guru.
> Exalted is the service of the True Guru,
> brother, to hold in remembrance the divine
> Name.
> God himself offers grace and mystic union.
> Worthless sinners are we, brother, yet the
> True Guru
> has drawn us to blissful union.[25]

The passage left no doubt as to whose side the Guru was on. The reference to the worthless and sinners was seen to apply to those who had suffered the humiliation and degradation of the caste system. The traditional Sikh leadership, in acknowledgment of the Guru's voice, opened the doors of the Golden Temple to the newly converted outcastes.

CONCLUSIONS

Given that this book has been conceived of as a comparative exercise—alongside the Sikh materials we are looking at other major world religions—I think it is worthwhile to conclude with some comparative propositions, particularly as they relate to Indic religious culture.

First, unlike Hinduism, where the sacred revelation, enclosed under the term *shruti*, could not be heard by members of all castes and was exclusively reserved for the upper castes or the so-called twice-born, the *Guru Granth Sahib* was open for recitation and transmission by all. While this proposition may not be of any grand consequence in the world we live in today, historically speaking this was a major rupture with tradition in the Indian context. The French anthropologist Louis Dumont has persuasively argued that the organizing principle of Indian society is social inequality.[26] If we accept this thesis, then we have to concede that the social order with deep divisions between the Brahmans and the outcastes was at least in part legitimized through scriptural resources. This is why only some could read and recite the scriptures, while others were barred from doing so. This exclusive way of looking at the world collapses with the inclusive spiritual worldview of the Sikh scripture.

Second, classical Hindu tradition was deeply suspicious of committing the sacred word to writing. Given the power and mystery inherent in the sacred word, this stance is to some extent understandable. The oldest corpus of Hindu sacred materials—the Vedas—was not committed to writing until the nineteenth century. This is not true of the primary Sikh scripture. As I mentioned earlier, the *Guru Granth Sahib* was turned into a written document as early as 1604, and some form of it existed in manuscript form much earlier than that.

This whole question of writing and printing is closely tied to social organization. It is intriguing that although the Indians had at least two opportunities to take up the technology of printing, both were ignored. The first chance Indians had to learn about printing was in the eighth century, from Buddhist pilgrims who were visiting the subcontinent from China. The second chance was when the Portuguese came to the west coast of India in the sixteenth century. Perhaps printing was perceived as a threat by Indian elites. It would have meant that all of the cultural and educational resources in due course would become available to all members of society. Printing does tend to be disrespectful of social privilege. For the Sikhs the transition from written manuscripts to the printing press in the nineteenth century was an easy one.

Third, in terms of religious identity the Sikh scripture is a complex collection. Given our contemporary denominational labeling it may be hard to understand why the Sikh scripture, besides containing the writings of Sikh Gurus, also includes a considerable number of compositions by Hindu and Muslim saint-poets. There is no simple answer to this question. Intriguingly, from time to time even some Sikhs have been baffled by this religious inclusion across religious boundaries. In the early twentieth century a prominent Sikh leader, Teja Singh Bhasaur, in his puritan zeal wanted to exclude the non-Sikh writings from the Sikh scripture. Although he was not allowed to do so, his case tells us something interesting about this issue. Perhaps one way to conceptualize the heterodoxy of the Sikh scriptures is by acknowledging that in India religious boundaries were highly fluid, particularly in the premodern period. Our contemporary religious labels and the discourse of world religions had no cultural register in the Indian environment.

This brings me to my final point. My earlier three submissions were largely to do with dissimilarities between the Sikhs and others who live in the Indian subcontinent. However, there are also similarities. A striking one is how the Sikhs, much like the Hindus, have come to share a preoccupation with hearing and reciting the sacred word rather than on interpretation and intelligibility. There are two possible explanations for this. One, this response could have something to do with the Bhakti associations of Sikhism.[27] In the Bhakti movement the governing sentiment was about devotion to God and God's word rather than an intellectual response. In fact, the intellect was devalued for religious purposes. It was not seen as an aid to salvation. Second, one wonders if intelligibility as a response to the word is not merely an aspect of Christian reformation and should not be universalized, except, of course, when other traditions may launch their own movements of reformation.

Suggested Readings

Four complete translations of the *Adi-Granth* have so far appeared in English. They are Gopal Singh, trans., *Sri Guru Granth Sahib*, 4 vols. (Delhi: Gurdas Kapur & Sons, 1960-62); Manmohan Singh, trans., *Sri Guru Granth Sahib*, 8 vols. (Amritsar: Shiromani Gurdwara Parbandhak Committee, 1969); Gurbachan Singh Talib, trans., *Sri Guru Granth Sahib*, 4 vols. (Patiala: Punjabi University, 1984-90); and Pritam Singh Chahil, trans., *Sri Guru Granth Sahib*, 4 vols. (New Delhi: translator, 1992).

See also the following:

Hans, Surjit. *A Reconstruction of Sikh History from Sikh Literature*. Jalandhar: ABS Publications, 1988.

McLeod, W. H., ed. *Textual Sources for the Study of Sikhism*. Manchester: Manchester University Press, 1994.

O'Connell, Joseph T., et al., eds. *Sikh History and Religion in the Twentieth Century*. Toronto: University of Toronto, 1988.

Singh, Harbans, ed. *The Encyclopaedia of Sikhism*. 4 vols. Patiala: Punjabi University, 1992-98.

Notes

[1] For historical and sociological insights into the Sikh diaspora, see N. Gerald Barrier and Verne A. Dusenbery, eds., *The Sikh Diaspora, Migration and Experience beyond Punjab* (Columbia, S.C.: South Asia Publications, 1989).

[2] This essay appears in Mark Juergensmeyer and N. Gerald Barrier, eds., *Sikh Studies, Comparative Perspectives on a Changing Tradition* (Berkeley: Graduate Theological Union, 1979), 13-23.

[3] A vast literature is available on the life and thought of Guru Nanak. Two excellent works that could help an initial reader are W. H. McLeod, *Guru Nanak and the Sikh Religion* (Oxford: Clarendon Press, 1968), and J. S. Grewal, *Guru Nanak in History* (Chandigarh: Punjab University, 1969).

[4] The most authoritative account of the *janamsakhi* literature is to be found in W. H. McLeod, *Early Sikh Tradition, A Study of the Janamsakhis* (Oxford: Clarendon Press, 1980).

[5] The following two works may be consulted on the evolution and consolidation of the Sikh tradition: Harbans Singh, *The Heritage of the Sikhs* (New Delhi: Manohar, 1985 reprint) and J. S. Grewal, *The Sikhs of the Punjab* (Cambridge: Cambridge University Press, 1990).

[6] Several books cover the history of Amritsar and its premier institution, the Golden Temple. A good start can be made by consulting Fauja Singh, ed., *City of Amritsar* (New Delhi: Oriental Publishers and Distributors, 1978) and Madanjit Kaur, *The Golden Temple, Past and Present* (Amritsar: Guru Nanak Dev University Press, 1983).

[7] The best source on this Guru's life is a biography by J. S. Grewal and S. S. Bal, *Guru Gobind Singh* (Chandigarh: Punjab University, 1967).

[8] On the critical importance of the Khalsa in Sikh history, see Harjot Oberoi, *The Construction of Religious Boundaries* (Chicago: The University of Chicago Press, 1994), 59-91.

[9] The five "K"s of Sikhism have drawn considerable attention. For an interpretive essay on this aspect of the tradition, see J. P. S. Uberoi, "The Five Symbols of Sikhism," in *Religion in India,* ed. T. N. Madan (Delhi: Oxford University Press, 1992), 320-34.

[10] See W. H. McLeod, *Guru Nanak and the Sikh Religion* (Oxford: Clarendon Press, 1968), 8, 153.

[11] Christopher Shackle, *An Introduction to the Sacred Language of the Sikhs* (London: University of London, 1983). This volume can also serve as an excellent resource to learn and master the language of the *Adi-Granth.*

[12] *Adi-Granth,* 1035 (standard pagination); *The Sikhs,* trans. W. Owen Cole and Piara Singh Sambhi (London: Routledge, 1978), 71, hereafter referred to as *The Sikhs.*

[13] *Adi-Granth*, 1037, translation in *The Sikhs*, 71.

[14] For instance, this argument is fully developed in Harold Coward, *Sacred Word and Sacred Text* (Maryknoll, N.Y.: Orbis Books, 1988). See also Wilfred Cantwell Smith, *What Is Scripture? A Comparative Approach* (Minneapolis, Minn.: Fortress Press, 1993), 166.

[15] William A. Graham, *Beyond the Written Word: Oral Aspects of Scripture in the History of Religion* (Cambridge: Cambridge University Press, 1987), 32-33.

[16] *Adi-Granth*, 152, translation adapted with minor modifications from *The Sikhs*, 75.

[17] *Adi-Granth*, 597, translation adapted with minor modifications from McLeod, *Guru Nanak and the Sikh Religion,* 193.

[18] *Adi-Granth*, 349, translation from *The Sikhs*, 95.

[19] *Adi-Granth*, 305-6. The term *Gursikh* is used for one who is attuned to the teachings of the Guru.

[20] Tara Singh Bains and Hugh Johnston, *The Four Quarters of the Night* (Montreal: McGill-Queen's University Press, 1995), 7.

[21] Hew McLeod, *Sikhism* (London: Penguin Books, 1997).

[22] See J. S. Grewal, *The Sikhs of the Punjab* (Cambridge: Cambridge University Press, 1990), 118-19.

[23] R. Nicholas and R. Inden, *Kinship in Bengali Culture* (Chicago: University of Chicago Press, 1977), 37.

[24] The prescribed hymns are the following collections: *Japji*, *Jap*, the ten *Savvvayyas*, *Benati Chaupai*, and the six prescribed stanzas from *Anand Sahib*.

[25] *Adi-Granth*, 638, as translated by W. H. McLeod in *The Evolution of the Sikh Community, Five Essays* (Delhi: Oxford University Press, 1950), 68.

[26] Louis Dumont, *Homo Hierarchicus: The Caste System and Its Implications* (Chicago: University of Chicago Press, 1980).

[27] For a recent statement on the Bhakti movement, see David N. Lorenzen, ed., *Bhakti Religion in North India: Community, Identity, and Political Action* (Albany, N.Y.: State University of New York Press, 1995).

6

The Dilemma of Authoritative Utterance in Buddhism

Eva K. Neumaier

THE DILEMMA

The authority of a Buddhist text or teaching is based on its claim that it authentically renders Buddha's word. Consequently, we should expect that all authoritative Buddhist texts begin with "Thus spoke Buddha," but there are no texts with such beginnings. The authoritative Buddhist text begins with "Thus I have heard" and then records the location and circumstances under which the speech now presented as text has occurred. In most cases the speech is attributed to Buddha Gautama, who is also known to the tradition as Shakyamuni, and whom modern scholarship likes to call the historical Buddha, the person with whom the history of Buddhism began.

While the Buddhist tradition makes the claim that the truth, the *dharma*, is contained, at least in some of these texts, and that, therefore, these texts are the *dharma*, it also claims that the *dharma* transcends all words and the capability of language. On the one hand, Buddhists have compiled hundreds of volumes of "canonical" Buddha word while, on the other hand, maintaining that all words are, at best, only approximations of the truth, and, at worst, altogether useless. This is one side of the dilemma of Buddhist scripture, which I will address in this presentation.

Another side of the dilemma is the historical finality of Buddha-word vis-à-vis its claimed metaphysical truth. The sheer amount of Buddha-word finds its historical boundaries in the time passed between enlightenment (when Buddha was in his early thirties) and his death (when he was eighty years old). Thus, one might conclude, there can be only a fixed number of Buddha-words. If this was ever true at all, then it was true only during the very early beginnings of the Buddhist traditions. As soon as concepts such as the universality of enlightenment and the all-pervasive nature of the Buddha-mind were postulated, the source of the Buddha-word was not exclusively invested in the historical Buddha and in his forty some years of teaching. To the contrary, anybody (and even things) animated by the Buddha-mind could utter Buddha-word. Thus, the dilemma is that, in theory, Buddhist scriptural texts should be closed and of a finite number, yet in reality they are open and constitute an ever-growing body of authoritative literature. A further aspect of the dilemma is that canonical Buddhist texts were often incorporated into what, due to lack of a better term, we call folk religion. I shall cite such an example toward the end of this chapter.

In order to shed light on these different aspects of the major dilemma, I shall first explain briefly what Buddhism is (always keeping in mind the main theme), then discuss the formation of the various canons and their differences and similarities, and finally deal with the problematic sides of Buddhist scripture in more detail.

WHAT IS BUDDHISM?

The Origins: The Buddha

Buddhism is the teaching based on the mystical experience of an Indian prince, known as Siddhartha Gautama, who lived approximately twenty-five hundred years ago. This prince became known to the world as Buddha, the Enlightened One.

In the jargon of scholarship this person became known as the historical Buddha. He was born into the Shakya clan, which ruled over an aristocratic republic in northern India (today part of modern Nepal). In search of spiritual truth, he, like many of his peers, left his family and social duties behind and wandered into the central Ganges Valley. After studying with several teachers he experienced a mystical transformation that had a lasting impact on his life. This is known as his enlightenment. He became a teacher himself, known as Buddha, which means the One Awakened to the Truth. For more than forty years he lived as a wandering ascetic and taught a following that aspired to the same experience as his. This is about as much as we know about Gautama Buddha as a historical person.

Fragments of biographical accounts are extant among the canonical texts, while autonomous biographies exist outside the canons. Each account renders a selection of events and presents them in a framework specified by certain interests. In these accounts Buddha did not claim to be the embodiment of any supernatural being. However, he did claim that he had rediscovered a truth that had been present in the universe since unknown times but which had vanished from the surface of the earth for some time. This truth is called *dharma*, a term varyingly rendered as "truth," "reality," "teaching," or "law." The Indic word indicates a system of thought that sustains and explains the nature of the universe, a theory one can "hold on to."

The *Dharma*

The truth *(dharma)* Buddha was to preach he found only after many years of futile attempts by practicing austerities almost to the point of suicide. Then, one dawn, Gautama had awakened to enlightenment. Nirvana, the mystical goal of Buddhism, had become a reality for him. Four insights dawned upon him:

- that life is suffering;
- that suffering is caused by desire;
- that if desire is dissolved, suffering will disappear and Nirvana will be realized;

- that there is a path toward this goal comprised of an ethics of nonviolence and respect, mental discipline, and insight.

Then he saw his own previous existences, the arduous path toward the present, and that *karma*, the influence exerted by his previous acts and thoughts, had shaped them. The same was true with regard to every other living being. Now, he knew, he had become an enlightened one, a Buddha. There would be no further life, no suffering, no death anymore.

For weeks Buddha, as Gautama was from now on known, remained in the vicinity of the bodhi-tree (a fig tree, now the center of the most prominent pilgrimage site of Buddhism in Bihar, India). He was convinced that no other human being would be able to understand what he had; it would be futile to teach, he concluded. But then god Brahma (a deity of the Hindu pantheon) approached him. Brahma pointed out that there were some humans who had already achieved considerable insight and who, if they received some further instruction, could actually achieve the same insight Buddha had realized. This argument convinced Buddha, and he decided to walk the 155 miles to Benares, the holy city of India, to teach. The first teaching happened north of the city in the Deerpark of Sarnath, where he met his first disciples, five ascetics who had lived with him before. With them Buddha shared his insight into the four aspects of truth (i.e, all life is suffering, suffering is caused by desire, the end of desire means the end of suffering, and there is a path to bring suffering to its end). For more than forty years Buddha crisscrossed the dusty roads of the Ganges valley teaching the *dharma*. This became known as "turning the wheel of the *dharma*." Whatever later generations of Buddhist practitioners thought the Buddha had taught during these forty years constitutes "the word of the Buddha." His following comprised ascetics, ordinary folk, kings, nobility, women and men.

When eighty years old, Buddha, together with a group of monks, was invited for a meal by Chunda, a smith. One of the dishes contained spoiled food, but only Buddha was aware of it. He prevented Chunda from serving the dish to anyone but himself. Soon afterward Buddha showed symptoms of food poisoning. His health began to deteriorate, and his disciples began reluctantly to espouse the possibility of their master's passing away. The account of Buddha's last days is a moving testimony to his deep humaneness and humility. When asked who should lead the community after his death, he answered that the *dharma* would be their leader and that each one of them had to be his or her own lamp.

THE "WORD OF THE BUDDHA"

The "word of the Buddha" was collected soon after his death, although the factual details of this gathering of material are unknown to us. A few centuries later the by then well-established monastic communities organized the tractates attributed to Buddha in systematically organized collections. These collections we call canons, as they contain the authoritative texts of Buddhism.

At an early time the problem arose for the tradition of what exactly constitutes the word of the Buddha. Buddhists more than anybody else were aware of the fleeting character of a spoken word. So what was commended to writing? The word spoken by the Buddha, or the word heard by the disciples, or the word most suitable for demonstrating the way to enlightenment; what hermeneutical devices were suitable to decipher the not always apparent meaning of a sacred text?

The Canons

There is not one canon of Buddhist texts that can claim sole authority. At the beginning of modern Buddhist Studies (early nineteenth century), a number of scholars thought that the canon written in the Pali language reflected the oldest and most authentic teaching of Buddhism. Consequently, one can sometimes read that the Theravada tradition, whose authoritative texts are those of the Pali canon, represents the oldest and most original form of Buddhism. But increased research over almost two centuries proved this assumption wrong. Each of the many canons preserves some aspects of Buddhist teachings that are not found in other canons while all canons do agree on some basic principles.

In the earlier parts of the twentieth century it was assumed that those ideas and stock phrases found in all canons could constitute a kind of "Ur-canon." However, this view proved unfounded when more details of how the early texts were collected and compiled became available.

General Observations

The circumstances under which the canonical texts were compiled lead us to the dilemma of authoritative texts *versus* oral narration. The crux of this issue lies in the manner in which Buddha used to teach and in the diversity and non-hierarchical nature of the early Buddhist communities. The texts as well as the tradition, both supported by non-Buddhist sources, tell us that Buddha embraced a pragmatic teaching method. In one of the texts he compared himself to a healer who administers a medication specifically designed for a particular person suffering from a particular illness. He had no panacea to offer. Thus, to brahmins he talked in their jargon by adopting terms, such as *brahman* or *atman*, but would fill them with a new, that is, Buddhist meaning. Wherever Buddha went, he met a new audience that required a different way of teaching. Only one person accompanied Buddha on all his wanderings—Ananda, his cousin.

The Buddhist traditions maintain that during the year following Buddha's death the monastic community came together under the leadership of Kashyapa, one of the most senior and highly respected monks, to collect the master's discourses. This event is known as the First Council. We have to ask whether all the monks and nuns from all the places where Buddha had taught (corresponding to today's Magadha, Bihar, and southern Nepal) came together, how the call for the meeting was disseminated, and if all were invited. We know that during Buddha's life the nuns claimed full membership in the community of Buddhist renunciates, but the tradition does not acknowledge their presence at the First Council. Modern scholarship has questioned the historicity of the First Council. If it happened at all, which is highly questionable, we have to conclude that only one part of the male monastic community came together to rehearse the master's discourses, while those communities that were not present at the council continued to transmit what they had received as the master's teaching as sideline traditions. Whether the texts these sideline traditions considered Buddha-word were ever put into writing to the same degree as those texts that the mainstream traditions approved as authoritative and authentic remains unknown to us.

The Pali Canon

The Pali canon is often considered the oldest and the one most likely to represent the original teachings of Buddha. This assumption is fostered by the Theravada traditions, which have become the custodian of the Pali canon.

Its claim to authenticity is based on the assumption that the word spoken by the Buddha was faithfully imprinted in the disciples' minds. Ananda, Buddha's attendant for decades, was equipped with an extraordinary memory, and so it became his task to rehearse the sermons after Buddha's entry into Nirvana. These sermons reproduced from Ananda's memory became the cornerstone of the Pali canon, which was put into writing after approximately three or four hundred years of oral transmittance. The text's authenticity rested at that time with the credibility of the rehearser. This became an issue already at the First Council, when Ananda was questioned about how he could remember the exact wording of Buddha's sermons although he had not achieved arhatship (full enlightenment). When Buddha's sermons started to proliferate in a number of Middle-Indian vernaculars, the problem of authenticity and faithfulness became more acute.[1]

But we have to be aware of the fact that the Pali canon as we know it certainly did not originate shortly after Buddha's death, nor was the collection put together the way we know it at the time of Emperor Ashoka (r. 272-36 B.C.E.). The date of Ashoka is important insofar as he left behind several lengthy rock inscriptions. In these inscriptions he quotes from Buddhist texts, some of which remain unknown to us, and he refers to collections of texts that do not correspond to the known organization of the Pali canon.

We know that by the fifth century the Pali canon had already taken on the shape familiar to us. Extensive quotes from the Pali canon as we know it are found in the opus of the Indian monk-scholar Buddhaghosa. He had become the main Buddhist thinker and writer in Sri Lanka around 500 C.E. To speak of a Pali canon prior to Buddhaghosa is risky, as it may lead to the assumption that the pre-Buddhaghosa canon is then viewed as identical with the one familiar to us, and nothing could be more wrong. With certainty we can say only that between Ashoka and Buddhaghosa the texts that make up the Pali canon were compiled and arranged in the present categories.

Other Indic Canons

Earlier we observed that certain collections of texts, all of them claiming to represent Buddha-word, circulated only within well defined geographical areas, thus leading to a significant geographical variation of what Buddhist communities considered "authoritative" texts.

It is the serendipity of history that the Pali canon fell into the custody of an orthodox and highly literary monastic community (the Theravadins), who preserved the canon very well once it had found its final shape. But this fact cannot deter us from acknowledging the existence of parallel Indic canons, although none was so well preserved as the Pali canon. We have only fragments of those parallel Indic canons. Later archeological finds yielded Buddhist manuscripts belonging to such a parallel canon and were safely dated as from the first century B.C.E.

Unlike other religions in which the religious institutions were very quick to eliminate ambiguity and plurality from the textual body, the Buddhist institutions did not intervene in the proliferation of parallel canons. To the contrary, from early times Buddhist texts and institutions affirmed this diversity by saying that there are eighty-four thousand forms of Buddhist teaching, and each can claim the same amount of authenticity as the others. The most significant change in the Buddhist understanding of what constitutes Buddha-word came with a movement that came to be known as Mahayana.

Redefinition of Scripture by the Mahayana Tradition

At this stage a segment of the Buddhist community, from which the Mahayana originated, felt the need to redefine the concept of scripture.[2] By that time the historical Buddha, whose paramount figure had dominated the early disciples' mind, faded away in favor of a symbolic understanding of Buddha's nature. In the words of Buddhist doctrine, we may say that the *dharmakaya*, Buddha's intrinsic awareness of reality, displaced the *rupakaya*, Buddha's visible presence or his historical existence. The word of the Buddha was no longer grounded in the earthly, historical Buddha's utterings but in its conformity with the spirit of what the historical Buddha had experienced, that is, enlightenment. Consequently, those who had achieved enlightenment could speak "in the spirit" of the Buddha. On this basis the Mahayana sutras claimed to be authentic scriptures, whether or not the words of the text had ever been voiced by the historical Buddha. But also the concept of what constitutes the content of the sacred text changed during this process of actualization. In the attempt to capture "things as they are" (one of the stock phrases of early Buddhist thought) the Buddhists found themselves in the predicament of having to express the inexplicable. Thus, Buddhist scripture changed from being a pragmatic instruction of how to achieve enlightenment (as expressed in the parable of the man hit by an arrow) to expressions of encountering a reality that was by its very nature beyond the reach of words (resulting in a language full of paradoxes and negations). Needless to say, the Buddhists following the "Saying of the Elders" (Theravada) strongly opposed such modifications to the concept of what constituted true scripture.

The hermeneutical device that made the incorporation of new ideas into the already existent body of scripture possible is known by the two terms *neyartha* and *nitartha*.The first term identifies a speech that needs to be "guided" toward its true and intended meaning, or whose meaning has to be "drawn out" from the words (this is the connotation of the Tibetan equivalent *drang don*), that is, a meaning which becomes transparent only through interpretation. The second term identifies a speech whose meaning has already been led to its goal of intended meaning and which for this reason is definitive. The classic source of this hermeneutical device is, according to the tradition, the *Samdhinormocana-sutra,* where the Buddha talks about scripture in need of interpretation *versus* one of definitive meaning.[3]

The Buddhist masters of the later Mahayana elaborated this device into a sophisticated hermeneutical system. For instance, Kamalashila, an eighth-century Buddhist master who spent much of his life in Tibet and who had an enormous impact on the formation of Tibetan Buddhism, saw the hermeneutical device of two categories of scripture in connection with the pursuit of enlightenment by means of wisdom and *bodhicitta* (mind of enlightenment). According to him, wisdom is nurtured in three ways: (1) through studying and learning *(shrutamayi),* which includes the study of the sacred texts in order to understand their intended meaning; (2) through intellectual investigation *(cintamayi),* which penetrates the befogged reality by means of logic and by reference to scriptural authority *(agama)* that may be of definitive meaning or in need of interpretation; and (3) through spiritual contemplation *(bhavanamayi),* which will integrate the truth found through logic and scriptural authority with its contemplative experience so that reality can be understood in its true being.[4] To rely only on one's intellect would be as wrong as to rely solely on scriptural authority.

This hermeneutical device enabled each stream of the tradition to acknowledge the sacred character of all the scriptural texts but reserved the label "scripture of explicit or definitive meaning" for those that were in accord with its own doctrinal stands. Thus all the branches or Schools of the Mahayana tradition agreed on the sacred nature of the texts that constituted the canon, but they disagreed on what texts contained the true meaning of Buddha's teaching. The subject of much debating between the various Mahayana traditions was then focused on which texts ought to be considered to be of definitive meaning and which are of peripheral meaning and in need of interpretation in order to make sense within the whole theoretical system of Buddhism.

The Translated Canons

When Buddhism began to cross the boundaries of the Indian cultural world to reach into the Far East, and later into the Tibetan Plateau, the need arose to translate the authoritative texts of Buddhism into the pertinent languages. But which were the authoritative texts? The foreign translators together with their Indian preceptors had to choose from this sea of parallel canons with their almost innumerable texts. Comparison of the Chinese canon, the oldest of all translated canons, with the Pali canon reveals that a certain number of Pali texts were incorporated into the newly formed Chinese canon along with a majority of Mahayana texts unknown to the Pali traditions.

These new texts taught a system of thought that, although rooted in ideas which were also found amid the Pali texts, was nevertheless innovative. It challenged several concepts that were held in high esteem among the Pali texts, such as the sacredness of the enlightened person *(arhant)*, the superiority of the monastic path, and so on. These new texts claimed to disseminate a "universal path" *(Mahayana)* suitable for laity and renunciates as well. The new and exciting spiritual ideal of the *bodhisattva* articulated a metaphysically conceived altruism and inclusiveness that was in sharp contrast to the rigid and self-centered asceticism of the Pali tradition.

We can plausibly assume that many of the narratives expressing the new ideas and ideals of the "universal path" were found either in the parallel canons of India or were transmitted as oral stories. But it is important to recognize that the Chinese translators together with their Indian mentors viewed these texts, oral or literary, as authentic Buddha-word and as authoritative. This situation implies that despite the emphasis Buddhist tradition put on strict and authentic transmission of the Buddha-word, it opened the body of its canonical works to a multitude of oral narratives. Without the impact of oral narratives and teachings, the Buddhist canons would present themselves in a very different shape and content than they do. Moreover, well-established canonical texts were often subject to a ritual use that had its undisputed origin in oral traditions, as I shall demonstrate later on.

Chinese

Buddhist rituals, icons, and later also thought became known in China from the first century of the common era on. They were transmitted via the oasis city-states along the silk road.

Thus, in the northern and northwestern parts of China a Buddhist tradition dominated that presented itself clearly in the garb of a foreign religion maintaining close ties with its roots in India and Central Asia. In contrast, in the southern parts of the country a more Chinese form of Buddhism developed that had less resemblance to its roots outside of Chinese culture. It sought to integrate the experience of enlightenment with traditional Chinese thinking. In general terms, the northern Buddhist tradition was more concerned with establishing a historically authentic body of Buddhist texts in translation, while the southern Buddhist tradition focused on exploring and realizing key themes of Buddhist mysticism. The search for the authentic body of Buddhist texts met with a "bewildering mass of diverse teachings that occasionally contradicted each other on essential points: thousands of scriptures of both Theravada and Mahayana origin; a great variety of scholastic treatises; monastic rules of different schools; sectarian texts and tantric rituals—all of which claimed to be part of Buddha's original message, and hence to be of impeccable orthodoxy."[5]

Chinese Buddhists developed two complementary approaches to deal with this bewildering variety of Buddhist texts and teachings. One response was to create a "graded revelation," that is, a scholastic system in which all teachings and texts have their contextually defined meaning and place. The believer moves through this maze of teachings and texts in the course of innumerable lives till eventually enlightenment is realized. The other approach was to synthesize the variety of teachings and texts into a mystical position, which in its most radical form denies the validity and use of textual studies. This second approach advocated a direct and spontaneous way to actualize enlightenment and rejected the literary scriptural tradition of Buddhism. The first approach resulted in the great scholastic systems of medieval Chinese Buddhism, while the second approach nurtured the fine arts and poetry and reached its pinnacle in Ch'an Buddhism (Japanese: Zen).

Tibetan

The academic concern with the Buddhist canon in Tibetan language dates back to the mid-nineteenth century when the

Hungarian explorer and pioneer, Csoma de Körös, brought the prodigious amount of Tibetan scriptures to the attention of the Western learned world. Shortly after the publication of Csoma de Körös's findings, the Royal Bavarian Academy of Arts and Sciences furbished two expeditions under the stewardship of the brothers Schlagintweit. Later, copies of the various editions of the Tibetan canon were acquired by the major research libraries in the West. After the exodus of many of the Tibetan monk-scholars from Tibet in 1959, more versions of the canon and supplementary collections of scriptures became available. These collections are the basis of our studies of Tibetan scriptures.

By the seventh and eighth centuries C.E., the time when the Tibetans came into contact with the Buddhist world of India and China, the emergence of Mahayana and Vajrayana scriptures had come to an end resulting in an undisputed supremacy of Mahayana (and to some extent also Vajrayana) scriptures. The Tibetans responded to Buddhism and its baffling variety of authoritative texts from within an ever-changing historic and cultural context. However, two main periods can be distinguished: the period of the Early Dissemination *(snga 'dar)* of Buddhism during the eighth and ninth centuries, and the period of the Later Dissemination of Buddhism *(phyi 'dar)* beginning in the eleventh century and coming to an end by the fourteenth century.

The inception of Buddhism in Tibet may have started with casual contacts between Tibetan tribes and the surrounding Buddhist nations. But not before the mid-eighth century did the existence of Buddhism in Tibet become a recognizable factor entrenched in the court culture. King Khri-srong lde-btsan (r. 755-797) became the main figure in introducing Buddhism into Tibet. But at this time only the royal family and some of the court nobles seem to have adopted this new religion. During his reign a number of documents appeared reporting the inauguration of Buddhism. Most of them refer only vaguely to Srong-btsan sgam-po, great-great grandfather of Khri-srong lde-btsan, as the king responsible for introducing Buddhism to Tibet. This evidence provided by the oldest texts is in striking disagreement with later Tibetan accounts, which see Srong-btsan sgam-po as the king who ushered in the Buddhist era. Up to the present no document, epigraphical or textual, has turned up that could claim with any amount of integrity to go back to the times of Srong-btsan. We have only documents that the tradition tells us were composed during the Khri-srong era, but even the oldest manuscripts do not go back beyond the tenth century. These documents point vaguely at a timid beginning of Buddhism prior to the era of Khri-srong.[6]

For the following discussion of the Early Dissemination I shall mainly rely on the information derived from the *sBa bzhed,* as it is the oldest report whose prime objective was to document the spread of Buddhism in Tibet.[7] Furthermore, its purported author is sBa gSal-snang, a member of the Tibetan aristocracy and confidant of Khri-srong. According to this document, sBa gSal-snang also played a major role in the dissemination of the teaching and was instrumental in drafting new legislation to implement the privileges of the Buddhist clergy in Tibet. This document has the promulgation of Buddhism under King Khri-srong lde-btsan start with a discovery made by Khri-srong's predecessor, Khri-lde gtsug-btsan (704-55). The *sBa bzhed* reports as follows:

> Homage to the three progenitors who gained control over the meat eating Red Faced [people] because they were divine embodiments of the three lords of buddha-families *(rigs gsum mgon po)*. (1.1)
>
> The edict has the words precisely written down: "When the mighty *(btsan po)* Khri-lde gtsug-btsan honoured the document of the last will of his forefather Srong-btsan at mChing-phu,[8] which, after minister 'Gar had inscribed [the king's words] on copper plates, was hidden there [Khri-lde gtsug-btsan] gazed [at these words]: 'At the times when my grandsons are called kings and nobles, the worthy and divine doctrine *(lha chos)* will come into existence. Renouncers of the home, barefoot and with shaved head, will follow the *tathagata*. They will wrap their bodies with the yellow robes [so that they look] like victory banners. Many of them will come to become an object of worship for gods and humans. To bring about happiness in terms of celestial rebirth and liberation for themselves and others, now and in the future, my grandsons as lords and ministers

> will [take care] that [the monks] be provided with a proper living by the Crown *(bla nas)*. For their happiness the subjects must carry [the burden of sustaining] those who are the object of worship by the Crown.' Such was written. [Khri-lde gtsug-btsan] was happy when he read [these words] as he thought 'I am the "lord" mentioned [in my forefather's will]' and he sent Bran-ka mu-le ko-sha and gNyags Dznya-na ku-ma-ra to India in the search of the doctrine (1.2-9)."

This paragraph makes it clear that Khri-lde gtsug-btsan, who was still a youth when he allegedly discovered his forefather's will in the archives of mChims-phu, felt a call to carry out a mission his forefather Srong-btsan was unable to perform because of the times being not "ripe" yet. We have to picture a scenario like this: the young prince, perhaps just recently enthroned (this happened at thirteen years of age), tried to familiarize himself with the administration and governance of the empire he had just inherited. He came across a document foretelling the growth of Buddhism, which at that time was the dominant religious system in Asia but perhaps only vaguely known in Tibet. The young prince interpreted the document to mean that he was called upon to fulfill his ancestor's prophecy. The young ruler grounded his legitimacy as leader of his people on the authenticity of the will and by assuming that the prophecy referred to himself. Hence, he saw himself as the fulfiller of the will of his forefather, the founder of the Tibetan empire. Consequently Khri-lde gtsug-btsan sent two young court nobles to India to "search for the doctrine."

The reason for introducing the doctrine is the advancement of happiness, which is the traditional objective of a Tibetan king. At present we have difficulty understanding what that phrase meant to an eighth-century Tibetan king. We may surmise that it meant prosperity and health for people and livestock but also protection from supernatural forces and dangers. The motivation for importing the Buddhist doctrine reads more like the search for an all-encompassing insurance policy rather than a search for enlightenment.

When the two Tibetan envoys had crossed into Indian territory, they heard of some Buddhist ascetics meditating at Mt. Kailash. They went to see them, and invited them to Tibet,[9] but the recluses refused the invitation, instead reciting to them two sutras *(Suvarna-prabhasottama* and *rNam par 'byed pa)*. The two Tibetans "invited" the sutras to Tibet, which meant they brought copies of the texts they had heard to Tibet. This indicates that between the time the two envoys heard the texts and the moment they entered Tibetan territory again, someone must have written down what the envoys had heard. Subsequently, the Tibetan king worshiped the texts and had five temples built to house the sacred texts.

In this report we hear nothing about the king or anybody else studying the sacred texts. They are worshiped and lavishly housed. In other words, the first reception of Buddhist scripture in Tibet was on the basis of their power to give presence to the divine, which reportedly should result in the establishment of happiness. Thus the sacred texts were in high regard not because of their message (which is the reason usually given in Buddhist tradition) but because of their assumed supernatural power to evoke and embody the divine presence.[10] Although the king was not very successful in his endeavor to establish Buddhism in Tibet, he instilled the same sense of mission in his son who was described as an extraordinary prince. When his father died prematurely, the young prince had to take over the governance of the country.

After resolving problems related to his own tender age, the prince assumed power and became a promoter of the Buddha teaching *(rgyal bu chos byed par 'gyur ro)*. At the same time, Shang-shi, who had been sent by the old king to acquire Buddhist texts in China, was about to return from his trip. When, during this journey, Shang-shi and his companions arrived at Wu-t'ai-shan, a famous Manjushri sanctuary, in a vision he saw Manjushri, who gave him a book. But when Shang-shi was about to return to Tibetan territory, he heard about anti-Buddhist riots instigated by some noblemen. To avoid persecution, Shang-shi hid the books in a cache near the Chinese-Tibetan border. Later, Shang-shi managed to get the books into Tibet, where they were translated into Tibetan. Approximately at the same time, sBa gSal-snang was sent to India on a mission to collect Buddhist manuscripts there and to invite Shantarakshita, a highly respected Indian Buddhist master, to Tibet. Later both Shang-shi and sBa gSal-snang traveled together to China.[11]

With the advent of Padmasambhava religious activities like the submission of local demons and their conversion to guardians of Buddhism, the construction of Buddhist statues and temples were of concern. Only after the inauguration of the first Tibetan monastery at bSam-yas (approximately 790 C.E.) and the ordination of seven Tibetan young men as monks did the translation activity gain prominence over other religious activities. Sacred texts imported from China as well as from India were translated into the native idiom with the assistance of Chinese and Indian scholars. This ambitious undertaking was financed by the Crown. The result of this translation activity was the production of a library of individual Buddhist texts housed in the royal palace. The individual Buddhist masters, whether Chinese or Indian, decided which texts they deemed suitable for translation into Tibetan. Thus the selection of Buddhist texts available in Tibetan by the late eighth century reflected the doctrinal predilections of these masters.[12] As far as we know, there was no attempt made to translate a complete set of the *tripitaka*. This did not happen before the period of the Later Dissemination.

The early period of Buddhist growth came to an end with what the tradition calls the persecution of Buddhism by gLang-dar-ma, the last of the Tibetan kings, who was killed by a Buddhist ascetic. A thorough examination of the pertinent sources seems to indicate that gLang-dar-ma was a more complex figure than later Tibetan records want to admit. Nevertheless, by the mid-ninth century C.E. the lavish royal patronage of Buddhism came to an end. For about a century Buddhism seemed to have almost vanished from the Tibetan scene. To what degree Buddhism became defunct was a matter constantly debated by early Tibetan scholars, and later by scholars of the Western world.

The later period of Buddhist propagation was inaugurated by the efforts of Rin-chen bzang-po a native of Guge (958-1055), a petty kingdom nestled in the western Himalayas. Rin-chen bzang-po undertook three strenuous journeys to India to gain a proper Buddhist education and to collect as many Buddhist manuscripts as he could. Generously supported by the king of Guge, Rin-chen bzang-po translated during his long life more than 140 texts from Sanskrit into Tibetan. When he passed away, hundreds of sacred texts had been translated into Tibetan for the first time and many of the "early translations" had been revised or retranslated.

At the time when Rin-chen bzang-po toured India, the political climate had dramatically shifted from the serene but relaxed and somewhat luxurious atmosphere characteristic of the late Gupta era—the period of the Early Dissemination—to an atmosphere of existential uncertainty. The main reason for this anxiety was the emerging of a new, violent political force in the Near East: Islam. India was paralyzed at the virulence of the Afghans' raids into the Punjab. They had become relentless promoters of Islam and were committed to converting the "infidels" by means of the sword. Millenarian movements sprang up to give reassurance to the believers who felt threatened in their human existence. Hinduism as well as Buddhism created figures of saviors who would come at the end of time to crush those forces that inflicted so much suffering on their people. From the eleventh century on, India was certainly in an "end time" mood. The Buddhist community, the prime target of the Muslims' attacks, saw the dusk of Buddhism coming. Thus, the Tibetans who came to India at that time tried to save of Buddhism whatever they could. The attempt to compile a complete set of Buddhist scriptures was a natural response to that situation. The motivation for adopting the full range of Buddhist teaching was to gain a complete knowledge of the entire tradition. Tibetans wanted to become experts in the *dharma*, which was so much endangered in its native India. The literary sources of Buddhist thought had to be translated and saved, but these much-famed translators had little or no interest in recording oral traditions.

The Tibetans looked for prophecies indicating that they would now be the heirs of the Buddha's teaching. Tibetan rulers saw themselves as embodiments of *bodhisattvas,* called upon to reinstate the Buddhist law upon earth. Texts like the *Manjusrimula* were translated and served as legitimization of the ruler's claim to promote Buddhism. Shortly after Rin-chen bzang-po's death a council was held in the capital of Guge, where tens of thousands of Buddhist scholars and monks congregated to revise the translated scriptures and to debate their dissemination. A flurry of scholarly activity resulted from this council. Tibetans learned to rely on themselves in their pursuit of Buddhist wisdom, because there were ever fewer Buddhist masters in India. Thus, the compilation of the Tibetan canon is a direct result of the political changes in India and the beginning of the demise of Buddhism there.

While during the Early Dissemination individuals of the Tibetan nobility were attracted to individual Buddhist masters, who introduced them to individual paths of enlightenment, during the Later Dissemination a community of Tibetan scholars made every effort to secure a firm textual basis for their further study and practice of Buddhism. During the early period Tibetans felt assured that in their pursuit of Buddhist wisdom they could rely on the limitless resources of Indian and Chinese Buddhism, but by the later period they knew that the days of Buddhism in India were numbered, and that Chinese Buddhism had lost its influence altogether by the mid-ninth century. While the motivation for adopting Buddhist texts during the early period was more a ritualistic and cultic interest, during the later period the Tibetans' motivation shifted to a more scholarly and text-bound interest.

As a consequence of these developments, the Tibetans established monasteries as major centers of learning, such as the monasteries of Zhva-lu and sNar-thang. There the numerous translations of Buddhist scriptures were collected. By the fourteenth century the Tibetan scholar-monks began to compile these individual scriptures into an authoritative collection, the first Buddhist canon in the Tibetan language. First, the texts were preserved in the form of manuscripts. Later, by the beginning of the fifteenth century, the Tibetan canon was printed for the first time, not in Tibet, but in China. The printed versions proliferated and branched into various "trees" or *stemma*.[13]

The Buddhist communities of Tibet were rather silent about which texts should be incorporated as authoritative and which should be excluded. This question was left in the hands of a few "experts," monk-scholars of unchallenged reputation in the eyes of their peers, like Bu-ston, who became the chief editor of the Tibetan canon. Among these scriptural experts heated debates were conducted as to which scripture is authoritative and which not. Attacks and counterattacks were launched, and many "refutations" were written in the attempt to discredit opponents' arguments. But the Buddhist community in general, including most of the clergy, remained detached from these issues. For most Tibetan Buddhists, scripture was what one's own teacher and his tradition had defined as scripture. Not the written version of the text but its recitation by a spiritual master was the source of religious illumination. The physical presence of the text was viewed as a dead shell that came to life only when read or chanted aloud.

In short, the selection of sacred texts incorporated in the Buddhist canon as compiled in Tibet during the fourteenth century was the product of a number of factors:

- Availability of the "originals" either in India or China;
- Change of the political situation in India and China, and the decline of Buddhism there;
- Severance of the ties with China;
- Doctrinal affiliation of the Buddhist masters teaching in Tibet;
- Needs of the Tibetan royalty to define their position as patrons of Buddhism;
- Political pressure issuing from the patrons of the chief compilers; and
- The necessity to incorporate local and oral Tibetan beliefs in Buddhist texts.

Scripture Embedded in Oral Tradition

Above I have indicated several times that even the most authoritative texts were, under certain circumstances, subject to a ritual use that was undisputedly rooted in oral traditions. I shall give here only one example for such use. The text under discussion is the *Heart Sutra*, one of the most revered Mahayana texts.[14] It epitomizes the Mahayana teaching of emptiness, that is, that the very nature of all that exists remains ineffable. Thus, it is a highly philosophical text, which in its dense technical language forms an enigma for most uneducated Tibetan peasants, nomads, and lowly clergy. Nevertheless, it is this text that is used as a potent charm to repel demons. The Tibetan text begins with a three-part introduction. The first part consists of a list of names beginning with the "perfect Buddha" in an attempt to give the text a semblance of authenticity. The second part is called "a history to inspire belief." In spite of its subtitle, this part relates a gruesome story of magical killings, of necromancy, and of subduing a demon of the "king" category *(rgyal po)*. The third part instructs how to set up the sacrificial site: in the center is a Buddha image surrounded on all four sides with figurines of the demon to be repelled and of various animals (that is, substitutes for real sacrificial animals). The officiating ritualist then enters a standard Buddhist meditation ritual by identifying himself with Buddha and offering to the Buddha the traditional offerings of water, flowers, incense, light, perfume, and music. This part ends with a plea—"I beseech the four demons, their retinue and servants to turn away"[15]—followed by a repeated recitation of the *Heart Sutra*. The apotropaic nature of the ritual becomes apparent in the following incantation:

> By the power of the words of truth of the noble three jewels, may our enemy so and so today be summoned, liberated [killed], and his flesh and blood be eaten by the gods and demons of the world. May his consciousness be led into the *dharmadhatu*.[16]

The last sentence, while expressing hopes that the killed enemy will attain buddhahood, puts only a thin veneer of Buddhist rhetoric on an otherwise harsh rite of exorcism. The oral tradition, most likely dating back to pre-Buddhist times, appropriated here a most revered philosophical Buddhist text to an end that is hard to justify on grounds of Buddhist ethics.

While this view may be espoused by the scholar, the Tibetan practitioner in all regularity does not see a discrepancy between the philosophical content of the *Heart Sutra* and its use in an apotropaic rite. Oral folk tradition of exorcism and magical killing becomes seamlessly fused with a highly philosophical and canonical text, whereby the latter remains encased in its enigmatic technical jargon, making it suitable to be usurped as a "magical tool."

MULTIPLICITY OF THE *DHARMA*

As we have seen, the Buddhist canon as well as the *dharma* exist only in diversity and plurality. While one text and one system of Buddhist thought and practice may be the right path for an individual or one community (for example, Pure Land), the multitude of individuals requires a multitude of authoritative texts, of canons and of belief systems.

Closed Canon

The origin of Buddhist scripture is given in the finite numbers of discourses Buddha engaged in during his lifetime. This situation would entail the concept of a closed canon. Whatever was recoded as Buddha-word at the beginning of the Buddhist tradition constitutes the entirety of the scriptural tradition. Nothing can be added and nothing can be deleted. But the hermeneutical device of "implied meaning" and "direct meaning" opened the door to an ongoing reinterpretation of what is an authoritative text and to theoretical and philosophical innovations.

Open Canon

If the theoretical claim of a "closed canon" of Buddha-word is put aside and if actual textual traditions are studied, the conclusion that the Buddhist canons are of an open nature is inevitable. For far more than two thousand years the Buddhist communities have rewritten their canons. Besides the literature encased in collections that can be called canons without question, Tibetan communities created secondary canons that often superseded the traditional canons in terms of their importance in daily practice, belief, and ritual. One of these secondary canons is of particular interest for our inquiry.

Visionary Revelations

Once the primary canon took shape in Tibet, which incorporated mainly texts of Indian origin, visionary texts appeared, which in the course of time formed a secondary canon. I am talking about the *gter ma* texts (revealed or discovered texts and teachings) collected in the *Rin chen gter mdzod* (Precious Trove of Treasure [Texts]) and similar collections *(Mani bka' 'bum* and *bKa' thang sde lnga)*.

The general and most visible characteristic of these Treasure texts *(gter ma)* is the claim made by the tradition that they were composed during the period of Early Dissemination and then hidden because "the time was not yet ripe" for their teachings. After resting in their hiding place (a cave, the hollow core of a statue, the attic of a temple, and so on) for centuries, a Treasure Discoverer *(gter ston)* becomes aware of the hidden Treasure through either dreams or visions that draw his attention to ancient prophecies attributed to Padmasambhava (a legendary figure of the eighth century). The Treasure Discoverer prepares himself (there are very few women among Treasure Discoverers) through meditation, rituals, and further visions to embark on discovering the Treasure and extracting it from its hiding place. In many cases the text found consists of a paper scroll that contains writings in a secret script. With the help of further visionary encounters, the script can be deciphered and is put into regular Tibetan.

Most of the Treasure texts contained in the *Rin chen gter mdzod* deal with complex tantric visualizations and rituals, while the texts contained in the *Mani bka' 'bum* and in the *bKa' thang sde lnga* contain quasi-historical hagiographies of the founders of the royal dynasty as well as other legends posing as history.

These quasi-historical narratives blend Buddhist thought with indigenous Tibetan narrative. One example is the hagiography of King Srong-btsan sgam-po. The text celebrates the king as an embodiment of *bodhisattva* Avalokiteshvara, whereby the divine *persona* of the *bodhisattva* totally absorbs the historical reality of a king who was a warlord and shrewd politician. Embedded in the Buddhist narrative of the *bodhisattva*-king's deeds is a narrative that most likely had existed among early Tibetans well before the founding of the empire (first half of seventh century). This narrative recounts how the first royal ancestor descended from the heaven to rule over the "black heads" (an old expression for the Tibetans), a narrative that exists also in a form not influenced by Buddhism at all. Thus, we may assume that the narrative of the ruler's descent from the heaven was an orally transmitted myth deemed important enough to be incorporated in the Buddhist genealogy of the most glorified Tibetan ruler.

THE WORD OF THE BUDDHA AS SILENCE

Denial of a Teachable *Dharma*

In general, Buddhists saw the final truth to be beyond words. Or, as G. Nagao once said, Buddha's silence is his foremost teaching. The vast majority of Buddhist authorities accepted the innate limitations of words and texts but insisted at the same time on their usefulness for guiding the believer along the path to enlightenment.

The Great Perfection: *Atiyoga*

Some sacred texts, however, explicitly deny the validity of any scripture. One such text is *The All Creating Sovereign, Mind of Perfect Purity (Kun byed rgyal po'i mdo)*. The *Kun byed rgyal po'i mdo* is a text found in the Kanjur section of some of the Tibetan Buddhist canons under the heading "Old Tantras," and also in two collections of tantras that were not universally accepted as authentic Buddhist scriptures, that is, the *Hundred Thousand Tantras of the Old Translations (rNying ma'i rgyud 'bum)* and the *Hundred Thousand Tantras of Vairocana (Bairo rgyud 'bum)*.[17] The *Kun byed rgyal po'i mdo* constitutes the main scriptural source of the "mind class" *(sems sde)* of the Great Perfection *(rDzogs chen)*, a mystical strand of the Old School of Tibetan Buddhism, which in its oldest literature bears close similarity with some Ch'an teachings.

Similar to the response of Chinese Buddhists to the multitude and variety of orthodox Buddhist texts, Tibetan Buddhists also developed complex theoretical systems to accommodate this variety and the often contradictory positions found in the authoritative texts. The Great Perfection tradition put its own teaching, Atiyoga, at the top of a nine-tiered system. This final stage is further divided into three segments: "mind class" *(sems sde)*, "expanse class" *(klong sde)*, and "sacred instruction class" *(man ngag sde)*. As already mentioned, the *Kun byed rgyal po'i mdo* belongs to the "mind class." The Tibetan tradition knows of eighteen texts of the "mind class," but there is widespread disagreement as to which texts belong to this group. The Old School accepts the Tibetan *tripitaka* supplemented with the *Hundred Thousand Old Tantras (rNying ma'i rgyud 'bum)* and the *Hundred Thousand Tantras of Vairocana (Bairo rgyud 'bum)* as its authoritative texts.

The main idea presented in the *Kun byed rgyal po'i mdo* is that existence is a manifestation of pristine awareness that is the intelligent ground of everything. This is referred to as "all creating sovereign" or "mind of perfect purity." The text then argues that because existence *is* divine presence, nothing can be achieved (negation of Nirvana), there is no spiritual progress (negation of the path), no good acts (negation of causes), no Buddha, no doctrine, and no disciples. This clearly constitutes a scripture denying the validity of scripture. In the following we shall see how the text argues for this paradox. The "mind of perfect purity" speaks as follows:

> I, as [the mind of] perfect purity, the actuating essence of all that is pure, let emerge from Me the play *(rol pa)* of the threefold world, and the six categories of sentient beings, because I am actuating the dimension of the non-conceptual, and I am the existential ground *(gnas chen)* of all Buddhas. Particularly I am teaching that, if you are not mistaken about the pure, all acts of happiness and misery are My compassion. I, the All Creating, will not teach such lore to those who adhere to the vehicle of cause and result. If I would teach them My lore as definitive they would cast praise and slander on Me, the All-Pure, as they assert that cause and result do exist because of good and bad acts. For this reason they will not meet Me, the All Pure One, for a long time. I am the teacher, the All Creating One, the

> mind of perfect purity. The mind of perfect purity is the All Creating Sovereign.[18]

The audience addressed here are those who do not follow the vehicle of causation, which is commonly understood as identifying the vehicle of the solitary Buddhas *(pratyekabuddha)*, the vehicle of the hearers *(shravaka)*, and the vehicle of the *bodhisattvas* (that is, Mahayana). Thus we may conclude the audience will consist only of the followers of the Vajrayana, which is usually referred to as the vehicle of fruition. On many occasions the *Kun byed rgyal po'i mdo* repeats that those who are addicted to the concept of causality will inevitably fail to grasp the lore of the mind of consummate purity because they are used to consider certain things as good and desirable while other things they see as bad and undesirable. But from the vantage point of the intelligent ground all things are equally pure, sacred, and consummate. Thus, to make such distinctions constitutes a denigration of the ultimate. The *Kun byed rgyal po'i mdo* presents itself here as the final and definitive teaching that renders all other scriptures superfluous.

The denial of the path to enlightenment, which is the soteriology of Buddhism, is explicit in the following:

> It is a great sickness to enter the path, which is [in reality] no-path. Those who wish to proceed on it are like a deer pursuing a mirage. [Abiding in stillness] is not an object of gain, nor does it arise from the threefold world. A state where they gaze at the ten *bodhisattva* stages is an obstruction of perfect purity.[19]

The ten *bodhisattva* stages mentioned here make up the entire path of the ordinary person toward buddhahood and enlightenment. To be concerned about this path and to aspire to it is called in this text an "obscuration," a term in other Buddhist texts reserved for those severe impediments that prevent the person from progressing on the path to enlightenment. Here, the *Kun byed rgyal po'i mdo* denies the validity of the entire Buddhist teaching. The *dharma* turns into a no-*dharma*.

This text advocates a no-action approach to realize a mystical transmutation:

> As there is no perceiving of objects, nor rejecting or accepting them—nothing, it is only perfected in the oneness of stillness. Then you are totally separated from the regulations and vows and the acts [required for] observing them.[20]

Ch'an / Zen Buddhism

When the Ch'an tradition began to take shape in China, the general authority of canonical texts was affirmed, but they took second place vis-à-vis the more important oral instructions of one's teacher. Tsung-mi gave the following distinction:

> "Doctrinal Buddhism" consists of the *sutras* and *shastras* left to us by the Buddhas and *bodhisattvas*, while "Chan" refers to the sayings and the *gathas* of our own spiritual compatriots. In contrast to "doctrinal Buddhism," which covers all the living beings in the entire universe, the *gathas* of Ch'an are very concise and effective in teaching one sort of person.... Texts, such as "Extended Biographies of Eminent Monks" contained oral instructions "uttered in different specific situations. Such a record would constitute a 'handle' by which its readers could grasp the truth."[21]

When the Ch'an tradition began to view the utterances of its own masters as superior means to guide disciples toward enlightenment, it de facto redefined what constitutes scripture in Buddhism. Without the "handle" of the oral utterance, one cannot "take hold of" enlightenment. With this move, the Ch'an tradition put the canonical texts into a position secondary to their masters' oral and often poetic utterances while, at the same time, not denying the authority and authenticity of the canonical texts.

CONCLUDING THOUGHTS

What began as an oral tradition, when the historical Buddha was engaged in spiritual discourse with people from all walks of life, made a huge detour through a bibliophilic obsession that resulted in thousands of volumes of authoritative texts, all claiming authenticity as Buddha-word. But this bibliophilic religion reverted, at least in some traditions, to recording the oral sayings of outstanding and exemplary individuals. At the same time, the fixed canonical text, regardless of its philosophical or ethical content, could be usurped as a magical tool in a religiosity that fused the scholastic and mystic side of Buddhism with a need for protection from unknown dangers in the forms of enemies and demons. The obvious dissonance between the various "uses" of authoritative texts in the Buddhist traditions found its reconciliation in affirming the ineffability of existence. While one may expect that once this ineffability was affirmed, the literary production would have come to a halt, the opposite was true. Because existence is ineffable, the distance between a text seen as authoritative by an informed community and a vision or dream of an often vaguely learned individual diminished. Thus, the proliferation of canons produced a philosophy claiming the ineffability of reality that opened a previously closed canon to incorporate visionary texts.

Suggested Readings

Lopez, Donald S., Jr., ed. *Religions of Tibet in Practice*. Princeton Readings in Religions. Princeton, N.J. : Princeton University Press, 1997.

Queen, Christopher S., and Sallie B. King, eds. *Engaged Buddhism: Buddhist Liberation Movements in Asia*. Albany, N.Y.: State University of New York Press, 1996.

Robinson, Richard H., and W. Johnson. *The Buddhist Religion: A Historical Introduction*. 4th edition. Belmont, Calif.: Wadsworth, 1997.

Samuel, Geoffrey. *Civilized Shamans: Buddhism in Tibetan Societies*. Washington and London: Smithsonian Institution Press, 1993.

Strong, John S. *The Experience of Buddhism: Sources and Interpretations*. Belmont, Calif.: Wadsworth, 1995.

Notes

[1] These events are fully treated in the pertinent literature. More information on this subject is given in Lewis Lancaster, "Buddhist Literature: Its Canons, Scribes, and Editors," in *The Critical Study of Sacred Texts*, ed. Wendy D. O'Flaherty (Berkeley: Graduate Theological

Union, 1979), 215-29; Harold Coward, *Sacred Word and Sacred Text: Scripture in World Religions* (Maryknoll, N.Y.: Orbis Books, 1988).

[2] Greg Schopen discusses the religious situation prevalent at the beginning of the common era in his article "The Inscription on the Kusan Image of Amitabha and the Character of the Early Mahayana in India," *Journal of the International Association of Buddhist Studies* 10, no. 2 (1987), 99-137.

[3] Lambert Schmithausen, *Alayavijnana: On the Origin and the Early Development of a Central Concept of Yogācāra Philosophy,* Studia Philologica Buddhica, Monograph Series IV (Tokyo: The International Institute for Buddhist Studies, 1987), 2:265 n.114.

[4] Kamalashila, *First Bhavanakrama*, in *Minor Buddhist Texts*, ed. and annotated G. Tucci (Rome: Istituto Italiano per il Medio ed Estremo Oriente, 1958), 2:198, 245.

[5] *Buddhism and Asian History,* ed. Joseph M. Kitagawa and Mark D. Cummings (New York: Macmillan, 1989), 140.

[6] The documents consist of an ancient fragment (edited, translated, and discussed by Hugh E. Richardson, "'The Dharma that Came Down from Heaven': A Tun-huang Fragment," in *Buddhist Thought and Asian Civilization: Essays in Honor of Herbert V. Guenther on His Sixtieth Birthday*, ed. Leslie S. Kawamura and Keith Scott [Emeryville, Calif.: Dharma Publishing, 1977], 219-29), a letter by Buddhaguhya (edited and translated by S. Dietz, *Ddie Buddhistische Briefliteratur Indiens: Nach dem tibetischen Tanjur herausgegeben, ubersetzt und erlautert* [dissertation, University of Bonn, 1980], 2:185-219), further discussion of the same letter by Eva K. Dargyay, "Srong-btsan sgam-po of Tibet: Bodhisattva and King," in *Monks and Magicians: Religious Biographies in Asia*, ed. Phyllis Granoff and Koichi Shinohara [Oakville, Ont.: Mosaic Press, 1988], 102-6), and the report written by sBa gSal-snang (*Une chronique ancienne de bSam-yas: sBa-bžed: Edition du texte tibétain et résumé français,* ed. R. A. Stein [Paris: Adrien Maisonneuve, 1961]).

[7] The so far oldest manuscript of the *sBa bzhed* was documented in 1997 through the joint efforts of the Tibetan Academy of Social Sciences and the Austrian Academy of Sciences. Hildegard Diemberger reported at the eighth Seminar of the International Association for Tibetan Studies, at Indiana University, Bloomington, Indiana, USA, that she is working on an edition of this manuscript. The newly discovered manuscript "presents considerable differences from the extant *sBa bzhed* versions in the mention of numerous historical details and in the narrative" (conference abstracts).

[8] Alternative spelling of mChims-phu, a place in Central Tibet where Khri-srong had an hermitage built (Giuseppe Tucci, *The Religions of Tibet*, trans. Geoffrey Samuel [Berkeley and Los Angeles: University of

California Press, 1980], 9). The place was a center of religious activity during the latter half of the eighth century.

[9] This bit of information implies that at the time this version of the *sBa bzhed* was composed or edited, Mt. Kailash was not considered to be part of *Bod* (Tibet) under the jurisdiction of the dynasty.

[10] Robert Detweiler, "What Is a Sacred Text?" in *Reader Response Approaches to Biblical and Secular Texts, Semeia* 31, ed. Robert Detweiler (Decatur, Ga.: Society of Biblical Literature, 1985), 222f.

[11] Stein, *sBa bzhed* (1961), 7-11

[12] A title list of this royal library is preserved under the name the *lDan dkar ma Catalogue*. Further evidence about which books existed by the eighth/ninth centuries in Tibetan is provided by the Tun Huang manuscripts.

[13] For discussion of this complex subject, see Helmut Eimer, "Some Results of Recent Kanjur Research," *Archiv für zentralasiatische Geschichtsforschung*, ed. Dieter Schuh and M. Weiers (Sankt Augustin, Germany: VGH Wissenschaftsverlag, 1983), fasc. 1; idem, "Preliminary Notes on Ngor chen's Kanjur Catalogue," *Tibetan Studies: Proceedings of the Sixth Seminar of the International Association for Tibetan Studies Fagernes 1992*, ed. Per Kvaerne (Oslo: Institute for Comparative Research in Human Culture, 1994), 1:230-36; Günter Grönbold, *Der Buddhistische Kanon, eine Bibliographie* (Wiesbaden: Otto Harrassowitz, 1984), 15ff.; Paul Harrison, "In Search of the Source of the Tibetan Bka' 'gyur: A Reconnaissance Report," in Kvaerne, *Tibetan Studies*, 1:295-300.

[14] Donald Lopez Jr., *Elaborations on Emptiness: Uses of the Heart Sutra* (Princeton, N.J.: Princeton University Press, 1996).

[15] Donald Lopez Jr., "Exorcising Demons with a Sutra," in *Religions of Tibet in Practice*, ed. by Donald Lopez Jr. (Princeton, N.J.: Princeton Press, 1997), 519.

[16] Lopez, "Exorcising Demons with a Sutra," 521.

[17] The Tibetan text is contained in the *Cone Kanjur,* vol. Dza 1b.1-92a.1; *Narthang Kanjur,* vol. Dza, 1b.1-120b.1; *Lhasa Kanjur,* vol. Dza 1b-123a; *Peking Kanjur,* vol. Dza (9), p. 93, 1.1-126.5.2; *Derge Kanjur,* vol. 97, 1b-86a; *rNying ma'i rgyud 'bum,* vol. 1, pp. 1-220, ed. Jamyang Khyentse; *Bairo rgyud 'bum,* vol. 1, no. 4, chaps. 58-84, pp. 384.1.1-435.5

[18] *rNying ma'i rgyud 'bum,* 1:17/18.

[19] Ibid., 1:76.

[20] Ibid., 1:132.

[21] Yanagida Seizan, "The 'Recorded Sayings' Texts of Chinese Ch'an Buddhism," in *Early Ch'an in China and Tibet*, ed. Lai Whalen and Lewis R. Lancaster (Berkeley: Asian Humanities Press, 1983), 188f.

About the Authors

Harold Coward is Professor of History and Director of the Centre for Studies in Religion and Society at the University of Victoria. His main fields are comparative religion, psychology of religion, and environmental ethics. He is a Fellow of the Royal Society of Canada and editor of *The Hindu-Christian Studies Bulletin*. His wide variety of publications includes *Pluralism: Challenge to World Religions* (1985), *Jung and Eastern Thought* (1985), *The Philosophy of the Grammarians* (1990), and *Derrida and Indian Philosophy* (1990).

Hanna Kassis is Professor Emeritus of Islamic and Near Eastern Studies in the Department of Classical, Near Eastern, and Religious Studies at the University of British Columbia. He received the Ph.D. in Near Eastern Languages and Literature from Harvard University in 1965. In addition to his *Concordance of the Qur'an* (1983) and its sequel *Las Concordancias del Corán* (1987), his articles focus on the revival of orthodoxy among Muslims, particularly in Muslim Spain and North Africa in the Middle Ages, and the Christian response to this revival.

Wayne O. McCready is an Associate Professor in the Department of Religious Studies at the University of Calgary. His research specialty is Second Temple Judaism and the origins of Christianity. He is the author of *The Function of Law in Second Temple Religious Parties and Sects.*

Eva K. Neumaier is Professor of Buddhist religion and literature in the Division of Comparative Studies in Literature, Film, and Religion at the University of Alberta, Edmonton. She received the P.Phil. and D.Phil.Habil. in Indian and Tibetan Studies from the Ludwig-Maximilians University, Munich, Germany, in 1966. Her work is in the area of Tibetan religion and literature. Her latest book is *The Soveriegn All-Creating Mind, the Motherly Buddha* (1992).

Harjot Oberoi is Professor of South Asian History at the University of British Columbia, Vancouver. He received the Ph.D. in social history from the Australian National University in Canberra. From 1987 to 1997 he occupied a chair in Sikh Studies at the University of British Columbia. He is the author of the award-winning book *The Construction of Religious Boundaries* (1994) and various essays and articles dealing with politics of identity, Sikh historiography, modern religious movements in South Asia, secularism, and religious fundamentalism.

Anantanand Rambachan is Professor of Religion at St. Olaf College in Minnesota, USA. He is the author of several books, book chapters, and numerous articles in refereed scholarly journals. His books include *The Limits of Scripture: Vivekananda's Reinterpretation of the Vedas* (1994); *Accomplishing the Accomplished: The Vedas as a Source of Valid Knowledge in Sankara* (1991), and *The Hindu Vision* (1992).

Eliezer Segal is Professor in the Department of Religious Studies at the University of Calgary. He received the Ph.D. in Talmud from the Hebrew University of Jerusalem in 1982. He is the author of *Case Citation in the Babylonian Talmud* (1990); *The Babylonian Esther Midrash: A Critical Commentary* (three volumes, 1994); and various chapters and articles dealing with aspects of Rabbinic literature, Jewish law, and comparative biblical exegesis.

Index

Abū Bakr, 75
Adi Granth: authority of, 128–29; compilation of, 119; as "guru," 120, 131–32; importance of the revealed word in, 125; reverence for, 113–15, 127; rites of passage and, 130–31; social inclusiveness and, 133; structure and language of, 121–23; use in everyday life, 4; written tradition and, 133
Āgamas, 97–98
aggadah, 21
Ahmadīs, 83n.16
'Alī (Muḥammad's cousin), 75, 82–83n.16, 83n.26
allegorical interpretation, 51
alphabet: Arabic, 74; Hebrew, 16, 26; Sikh, 122
Ananda, 143, 144
ancestral traditions, 20
apocalypses, 46
Apocrypha, the, 82n.14
Arabic language, 69–70, 81–82n.8
architecture, 55–56, 60
Arjan, 119
Arsha Vidya Pitham, 107
art, 51, 55–56, 60
Arya Samaj, 100, 106
Ashoka, Emperor, 144, 145
Athanasius, 83n.17
Atiyoga, 161–64
ātman, 104, 105
aurality, 49, 54
authority of scripture: in Buddhism, 138, 142–57; in Hinduism, 91–94, 112n.21; in Judaism, 20; in Sikhism, 128–29
āyah, 70–71, 72
āyāt, 76

Bains, Tara Singh, 126
basmalah, 76–77
Bhakti movement, 134–35
Bhasaur, Teja Singh, 134
Bhavagadgītā, 95–96, 100
Bible, the: conclusions regarding the relation of Christianity to, 59–60; Jewish classification of Hebrew, 24; monastic traditions and, 52–54; the Protestant Reformation and, 56–59; translation of, 9–10. *See also* New Testament; Old Testament; Torah, the
bKa' thang sde lnga, 160
bodhisattvas, 160, 163

brahman, 104, 105
brahmins, 92
Brahmo Sabha, 106
Buddha: biographical sketch of, 139–40; the *dharma* of, 140–42; scriptural authority and, 138–39; silence as the word of, 161–64; teaching method of, 143; various traditions' attitude toward the words of, 146
Buddhaghosa, 145
Buddhism: the canons of, 142–57; chanting and, 2–4, 8; dilemma of scriptural authority in, 138–39, 164–65; language as an obstruction in, 11–12; the multiplicity of the *dharma* and, 159–61; oral tradition and, 157–59; overview of, 139–42; silence and, 161–64
Bu-ston, 157

calendars, 21–23
Calvin, John, 57
canon: Buddhism and, 142–57, 159–61; Christian attitudes toward, 59–60; of the New Testament, 46–47, 48–49, 83n.17; of the Old Testament, 38–41, 82n.14, 82n.15; the Protestant Reformation and, 59; of the Qur'ān, 72–76
Ch'an Buddhism. *See* Zen Buddhism
chanting: Buddhism and, 2–4, 8; Christianity and, 5, 53; Hinduism and, 2, 93, 101–2, 109; Islam and, 5–6; Judaism and, 4–5, 26; Sikhism and, 4, 122
Chinese Buddhism, 148–49
Chinmaya Mission, 107
Chinmayananda, Swami, 107
Christianity: conclusions regarding scripture and, 59–60; memorization and, 7; the New Testament, the Christian devotee, and, 49–52; the Old Testament and, 38–43; oral recitation and, 5; origins of, 37–38, 43–48; overview of role of scripture in, 34–35; sermons, liturgy, architecture, and art in, 54–56; Sikhism and, 135
Clement of Rome, 47
commandments, the, 29–30
Constantine, 48
Coward, Harold, 88, 99

Dayananda Sarasvati, 100, 106, 107
Dead Sea Scrolls, 21, 22, 38, 43, 46
dharamsal, 118
dharma: multiplicity of, 159–61; overview of, 140–42; relation to texts, 138; as a secondary goal of Hinduism, 87; in Tibetan Buddhism, 163
Dumont, Louis, 133

Early Dissemination of Buddhism in Tibet, 150, 151–54
Ellul, Jacques, 9

Essenes, 37
Eusebius, 48

Fātiḥah, 68
Feast of Weeks, the, 16–19, 21–27
features of scripture, 35–37
First Council of Buddhism, 143–44

Ghulām Ahmad, Mirza, 83n.16
gLang-dar-ma, 154
Gobind Singh, 119–20
Golden Temple, the, 119, 127, 132–33
gospels, the, 45–46
Graham, William, 53–54, 124
Great Perfection tradition, 161–62
gter ma texts, 160
gurdwaras, 126–27
Gurmukhi, 122
Guru-Granth (doctrine), 129
Guru Granth Sahib. See *Adi Granth*
guru mantras, 7–8, 14n.8
Guru-Panth, 129
gurus, 87, 102, 119, 120, 131–32
Gutenberg, Johann, 56
Gutenberg Bible, 56

Ḥadīth, 70, 80n.1
Ḥafṣah, 75, 76
Hagiographa, 24, 32n.14
Halakhah, 21, 27–28
Handel, George, 51
Heart Sutra, 157–59
Hillel the Elder, 15–16
Hinduism: classification of texts of, 88–89; compared with Sikhism, 133–34; diversity of, 85–86; guru mantras and, 14n.8; the highest goal of, 86; memorization and, 7–8; oral recitation and, 1–2; overview of types of secondary scriptures in, 94–116; the Vedas and, 89–94; the *via negativa* and, 10–11
Hindu Society of Minnesota, 109
Holy Spirit, the, 10
hukam, 128
Hus, John, 57
Hussein, King, 63

Ignatius of Antioch, 47
illiteracy, 50, 99
Indic Canons of Buddhism, 145
individualism, 57
International Society for Kṛṣṇa Consciousness, 97
Islam: Arabic language and, 69–70; the canon of the Qur'ān and, 72–76; memorization and, 5, 7; Muḥammad on the core of, 80–81n.1; and the Qur'ān's structure, 70–72; the revelation of the Qur'ān and, 64–69; and the structure of *suwar*, 76–78; Tibetan Buddhism and, 155

Ja'far ibn Abī Ṭālib, 68–69
Jaimini, 112n.22
japa, 101–2
Jerome, 82n.13, 82n.14, 83n.17

Jesus: early Christianity's understanding of, 37–38; interpretation of scripture by, 44; Jewish scriptures and, 42; oral recitation of scripture and, 5
Jesus movement, the, 44
Jodo Shinshu Buddhism, 3, 8
Josephus Flavius, 20
Judaism: Christianity and the scriptures of, 41–42; Christianity's origins and, 37; dynamism of the oral tradition in, 30–31; examples of interplay of oral and written traditions in, 16–19; Hillel, the two Torahs, and, 15–16; and interpretation of the commandments, 29–30; lunar and solar calendars and, 21–23; the Midrash's role in, 23; Pharisees, Sadducees, and the ancestral traditions in, 19–21; recitation in, 4–5; Torah in the daily life of, 27–29; use of scripture in the synagogue in, 23–27
Juergensmeyer, Mark, 115

Kamalashila, 147
karma, 88, 141
kathās, 108
Khadījah, 65–66
Khalsa, 119–20
Khri-lde gtsug-btsan, 151–52
Khri-srong lde-btsan, 150–53
kingdom of God, 38, 44
King James Version of the Bible, 10, 49
kirtan, 118, 127
Klostermaier, Klaus K., 85
koans, 11
Körös, Csoma de, 150
Kun byed rgyal po'i mdo, 161–64

langar, 119
Later Dissemination of Buddhism in Tibet, 150, 154–57
lectionary cycles, 25–26
Leonardo da Vinci, 51
liberation, 87, 88, 118. *See also mokṣa*
Lipner, Julius, 106
literacy, 56–57, 99, 110
liturgy: Christian, 54–55; Judaic, 25–26; the Qur'ān and, 78–80; Sikh, 125–26. *See also* ritual
lunar calendars, 21–23
Luntshitz, Solomon Ephraim, 30–31
Lutgendorf, Philip, 109
Luther, Martin, 9–10, 57

Madhymika Buddhism, 11–12
Mahābhārata, 95–96
Mahayana Buddhism, 146–47, 148, 150
Maimonides, 30
Mani bka' 'bum, 160
mantras, 93, 101–2
Manu, 110
Marx, Karl, 129
master stories, 45
McLeod, W. H., 122, 128

memorization: Buddhism and, 3–4; contemporary lack of emphasis on, 6–8; Hinduism and, 92, 93, 99–100; Islam and, 5, 73–74; Judaism and, 4–5, 26, 32n.16; the Protestant Reformation and, 58; Sikhism and, 124, 125–26
messianism, 42
Methodism, 57
Michelangelo, 51
Midrash, 23
Miqra', 25
Mishnah, 21
modernity, 56–57, 129
mokṣa, 86, 87, 88, 105
monasticism, 52–54, 55, 156
Muḥammad: on the essence of Islam, 80–81n.1; memorization and, 5; the Qur'ān and, 64–69; and the *suwar*, 72
mukti, 118
Müller, F. Max, 92
Muratori, 48
music, 51
mythos, 45

Nagao, G., 161
nam-simran, 118
Nanak, Guru, 116–19
New Testament: canon of, 48–49, 83n.17; the Christian devotee and, 49–52; and the origins of Christianity, 43–48
Nirvana, 140

Old Testament, 38–43, 82n.14, 82n.15. *See also* Prophets, the (books of the Old Testament); Torah, the
Omar (second Caliph), 73, 75
oral tradition: Buddhism and, 157–59, 164–65; Christianity and, 50, 53–54; contemporary decline in the, of various religions, 6–9; the gospels and, 45–46; Hinduism and, 88–89, 92–94; Judaism and, 16–19, 23, 25–26, 28–29, 30–31; Luther and, 9–10; overview of the, of various religions, 1–6; the Protestant Reformation and, 58–59; the Qur'ān and, 73–74; the Rabbis and, 21; Sikhism and, 124–25; the two Torahs and, 15–16. *See also* chanting; liturgy; recitation
Origen of Alexandria, 51
Orthodox Church, 38, 39, 40, 52–53, 82n.14
Otto, Rudolf, 77

Pali Canon of Buddhism, 144–45, 148
Paul, St., 9, 82n.13
Pharisees, the, 19, 20, 37
Pietist movement, the, 57
pluralism, 41–42
poetry, 1–2
Polycarp of Smyrna, 47
Pramāṇa, 102–3
printing, 50, 56, 59, 60, 133–34
Prophets, the (books of the Old Testament), 24, 32n.14

Protestantism, 38, 39, 40. *See also* Reformation, the
Purāṇas, 97
Puritans, 10
Pūrva Mīmāṁsā, 91–92, 103–4

Qumranites, 37
Qur'ān: Arabic language and, 69–70, 81–82n.8; the canon of, 72–76; liturgical use of, 78–80; memorization and, 5, 7; Muḥammad and, 64–69; structure of, 70–72, 76–78

Rabbinic Judaism, 20, 41
Rabbis, the, 20–21
Rahit-Maryada, 126
Ramakrishna Mission, 106
Rāmānuja, 104–5
Rāmāyaṇa, 96–97, 107–10
Ram Das, 119, 125
Rāmlīlā, 107
Ranjit Singh, Maharaja, 129
recitation: Christianity and, 5; Hinduism and, 1–2, 99–100; Judaism and, 4–5; of the Qur'ān, 78–79; Sikhism and, 122, 126; the Vedas and, 93–94
Reformation, the, 56–59
relationality: Christian art and, 55–56; Christian monasticism and, 54; Christian scripture and, 60; between religious communities and scripture, 36
revelation: the Qur'ān and 64–67; Sikhism and, 120, 124–29; the Vedas and, 91
Rin-chen bzang-po, 154–55, 156
Rin chen gter mdzod, 160
rites of passage, 130–31
ritual: Hinduism and, 94, 100–101; Sikhism and, 130–31; Tibetan Buddhism and, 158
Roman Catholic Church, 38, 39, 40, 52–53
Roy, Ram Mohan, 106

Sabbath, the, 21, 25–26, 28–29
Sadducees, the, 20, 37
Sagar, Ramanand, 108
sahaj, 118
saṁsāra, 88, 118
sangat, 118–19
Śaṅkara, 92, 104, 105
Sanskrit, 93, 110
sBa bzhed, 151–52, 166n.7, 167n.9
sBa gSal-snang, 151, 154
Schlagintweit, the brothers, 150
scrolls, 25–26
Septuagint, 38, 53, 82n.13
sermons, 10, 27, 54–55, 58
Shackle, Christopher, 122
Shang-shi, 153–54
Shavu'ot, 16–19, 28
shema, the, 4
Shī'ah, the, 82n.16
Shinran, 3
Sikhism: anecdote of reverence for scripture of, 113–15; chanting in, 2, 4; compared with other religious traditions, 133–35; ethnography of rites of passage and the sacred text of, 130–33;

overview of, 115–21; the power of the revealed word in, 124–29
silence, 161–64
Singh Ragi, Darshan, 127
Singh Sabha, 129
Smith, Wilfred Cantwell, 36
smṛti, 88–89, 94–116
solar calendars, 21–23
sola scriptura, 57
Soleveitchik, J. D., 27–28
Soto Zen Buddhism, 11–12
Sri Guru Granth Sahib. See *Adi Granth*
Srong-btsan sgam-po, 150–51, 152, 160–61
śruti, 88–94
Stock, Brian, 131
Sunnīs, the, 82–83n.16
sūrah/suwar, 71, 72, 76–78
sūtras, 112n.21
Suyūṭī, 71, 74
symbols, 51
synagogues, 23–27, 32n.21

Ṭabarī, 65, 73
Tagore, Rabindranath, 99
Talmuds, 21
Tantras, 98
Targum, the, 26
television, 108–10
Theravada Buddhism, 142, 145, 146
Tibetan Buddhism: canon of, 149–50, 160–61; chanting in, 2–3; silence and, 161–64
Torah, the: Christianity's origins and, 37; the commandments and, 29; in daily life, 27–29; the Feast of Weeks and, 17–18; Hillel and the written and oral, 15–16; historical scholarship on the composition of, 24–25; lectionary cycles and, 25–26; oral tradition and the dynamism of, 30–31; relation to other books of Jewish scripture, 24; the Sadducees and, 20; treatment of scrolls of, 26–27; ways it is taught and read, 4
translation: Buddhism and, 147–57; Christianity and, 9–10, 40, 49–50; Hinduism and, 98–99, 110; Judaism and, 26, 27; the Protestant Reformation and, 58
Tsung-mi, 164
Tulasīdāsa, 108

Upaniṣads, 86, 90–91, 104, 105, 106
Uthmān, 71–72, 76

Vajrayana scriptures, 150, 163
vak, 128
vak lao, 4
van der Leeuw, G., 12
Vedāṇgas, 93–94
Vedānta school, 104–7
Vedas, the: authority of, 91–94, 112n.21; hesitancy to put in writing, 133; liberation and, 88; memorization of, 99–100; Pūrva Mīmāṁsā on,

103–4; structure of, 89–91; Uttara Mīmāṁsā school on, 104–7
vernacular, the, 58, 98–99. *See also* translation
via negativa, 10–11
vismad, 118
Vivekananda, Swami, 106
Vulgate, the, 48, 53, 82n.13

Wesley, Charles, 57
Wesley, John, 57
written tradition: Buddhism and, 164–65; Christianity and, 50; Hinduism and, 88–89, 99; Islam and, 74–76; Judaism and, 16–19, 23, 28–29; and a lack of awe toward scripture, 13; modern emphasis on, 9, 12, 124; the Protestant Reformation and, 58–59; Sikhism and, 133–34; the two Torahs and, 15–16
Wycliffe, John, 57

Yajñas, 101

Zayd ibn Thābit, 74, 75, 76
Zen Buddhism, 11–12, 164
Zwingli, Ulrich, 57

Other Titles in the Faith Meets Faith Series

Toward a Universal Theology of Religion, Leonard Swidler, Editor
The Myth of Christian Uniqueness, John Hick and Paul F. Knitter, Editors
An Asian Theology of Liberation, Aloysius Pieris, S.J.
The Dialogical Imperative, David Lochhead
Love Meets Wisdom, Aloysius Pieris, S.J.
Many Paths, Eugene Hillman, C.S.Sp.
The Silence of God, Raimundo Panikkar
The Challenge of the Scriptures, Groupe de Recherches Islamo-Chrétien
The Meaning of Christ, John P. Keenan
Hindu-Christian Dialogue, Harold Coward, Editor
The Emptying God, John B. Cobb Jr. and Christopher Ives, Editors
Christianity through Non-Christian Eyes, Paul J. Griffiths, Editor
Christian Uniqueness Reconsidered, Gavin D'Costa, Editor
Women Speaking, Women Listening, Maura O'Neill
Bursting the Bonds?, Leonard Swidler, Lewis John Eron, Gerard Sloyan, and Lester Dean, Editors
One Christ—Many Religions, Stanley J. Samartha
The New Universalism, David J. Kreiger
Jesus Christ at the Encounter of World Religions, Jacques Dupuis, S.J.
After Patriarchy, Paula M. Cooey, William R. Eakin, and Jay B. McDaniel, Editors
An Apology for Apologetics, Paul J. Griffiths
World Religions and Human Liberation, Dan Cohn-Sherbok, Editor
Uniqueness, Gabriel Moran
Leave the Temple, Felix Wilfred, Editor

The Buddha and the Christ, Leo D. Lefebure
The Divine Matrix, Joseph A. Bracken, S.J.
The Gospel of Mark: A Mahāyāna Reading, John P. Keenan
Revelation, History and the Dialogue of Religions, David A. Carpenter
Salvations, S. Mark Heim
The Intercultural Challenge of Raimon Panikkar, Joseph Prabhu, Editor
Fire and Water: Women, Society, and Spirituality in Buddhism and Christianity, Aloysius Pieris, S.J.
Piety and Power: Muslims and Christians in West Africa, Lamin Sanneh
Life after Death in World Religions, Harold Coward, Editor
The Uniqueness of Jesus, Paul Mojzes and Leonard Swidler, Editors
A Pilgrim in Chinese Culture, Judith A. Berling
West African Religious Traditions, Robert B. Fisher, S.V.D.
Hindu Wisdom for All God's Children, Francis X. Clooney, S.J.
Imagining the Sacred, Vernon Ruland, S.J.
Christian-Muslim Relations, Ovey N. Mohammed, S.J.
The Divine Deli, John H. Berthrong
The Meeting of Religions and the Trinity, Gavin D'Costa

Of Related Interest

Life after Death in World Religions

Edited by Harold Coward

ISBN 1-57075-119-6

Is there life after death? If so, what is it like?
How does it relate to life in this world?
Life after Death in World Religions retrieves classic responses from Buddhist, Chinese, Christian, Muslim, Hindu, and Jewish traditions and presents them with clarity and authority.

Thank you for reading
Experiencing Scripture in World Religions.
We hope you enjoyed it.